THE OTHER SIDE

A Teen's Guide to
Ghost Hunting
and the
Paranormal

THE OTHER SIDE

A Teen's Guide to
Ghost Hunting
and the
Paranormal

BY MARLEY GIBSON, PATRICK BURNS, AND DAVE SCHRADER

GRAPHIA

HOUGHTON MIFFLIN HARCOURT
BOSTON   NEW YORK   2009

FOR INFORMATION ABOUT PERMISSION TO REPRODUCE SELECTIONS
FROM THIS BOOK, WRITE TO PERMISSIONS, HOUGHTON MIFFLIN HARCOURT
PUBLISHING COMPANY, 215 PARK AVENUE SOUTH, NEW YORK, NEW YORK 10003.

GRAPHIA AND THE GRAPHIA LOGO ARE REGISTERED TRADEMARKS OF
HOUGHTON MIFFLIN HARCOURT PUBLISHING COMPANY.

WWW.HMHBOOKS.COM

THE TEXT OF THIS BOOK IS SET IN TIMES NEW ROMAN.
PHOTOS ARE FROM THE AUTHORS' PRIVATE COLLECTION UNLESS
OTHERWISE MARKED.

LIBRARY OF CONGRESS CATALOGING-IN-PUBLICATION DATA
GIBSON, MARLEY.
  THE OTHER SIDE : A TEEN'S GUIDE TO GHOST HUNTING AND THE
PARANORMAL / BY MARLEY GIBSON, PATRICK BURNS, DAVE SCHRADER.
     P. CM.
  ISBN 978-0-547-25829-4 (PBK.)
 1. PARAPSYCHOLOGY. 2. GHOSTS. I. BURNS, PATRICK. II. SCHRADER,
DAVE. III. TITLE.
  BF1031.G45 2009
  13—DC22

2009022500

MANUFACTURED IN THE UNITED STATES OF AMERICA
WOZ 10 9 8 7 6 5 4 3 2 1

DR. HANS HOLZER

1920–2009

TO THE ORIGINAL "GHOST HUNTER"
AND THE ONE WHO POPULIZED THE PHRASE
"THE OTHER SIDE." NOW YOU KNOW THE ANSWERS
TO THE MYSTERIES YOU STUDIED FOR MANY YEARS.
YOUR INFLUENCE IN THE WORLD OF PARANORMAL
RESEARCH CANNOT BE UNDERESTIMATED.
YOU WILL BE DEARLY MISSED.

AND TO OUR FRIENDS
KELLY AND BRETT FREESE,
OWNERS OF OUR FAVORITE HAUNTED HOTEL,
THE PALMER HOUSE IN SAUK CENTRE, MINNESOTA.
MAY YOU NEVER KNOW A DAY WITHOUT
HAPPINESS AND SUCCESS!

ACKNOWLEDGMENTS

Most "how to" books will often cite sources of information the authors have used in footnotes and the bibliography. In chapters where we borrow a direct quote, we will do the same. However, the three of us agree that because we have been engrossed in the paranormal for so many years, the exact sources of much of our knowledge or inspiration have become clouded by the passage of time. Therefore, we each wish to individually acknowledge those who have inspired us—in large or small part—along this journey.

MARLEY WOULD LIKE TO THANK THE FOLLOWING: First and foremost, Patrick Burns and Dave Schrader, my partners in paranormal crime. They are my teachers, my mentors, and my friends. Couldn't have done this book without them. Our editor, Julia Richardson, whom I took ghost hunting with me, so she knows what we're talking about and that we're serious about our investigations and advice. And to everyone at Houghton Mifflin Harcourt for letting us run with our idea to educate the next generation of ghost hunters and huntresses. Deidre Knight, my (our) agent extraordinaire and dear friend, who not only believes in what we're doing but also happens to have ghosts in her house and loves to go ghost hunting herself. Mike Gibson for his love and support over the years. He'll always be in my heart. Finally, psychic investigator Maureen Wood for letting me tap into the depths of knowledge and experience in her life and sharing it with others.

PATRICK WOULD LIKE TO THANK THE FOLLOWING: My family for nurturing my bizarre obsession with cemeteries at an early age. My sons, William and Alec, for their unconditional love and understanding. Pamela Burns for her support all these years. I truly would not be where I am today if it were not for her. My coauthor Marley Gibson for supporting me, even when I doubt myself. And for guiding me in the publishing world. My "brother" in the paranormal, Dave Schrader, for opening many doors of opportunity. Harry Houdini, an original debunker of fraudulent paranormal claims. James Randi, who has done an impressive job of picking up where Houdini left off. We don't always see eye to eye, but I'm thankful for the work James has done to weed out the bad apples. Hans Holzer, the man who coined the term "ghost hunter." I feel blessed to have met Hans in person. Dr. William Roll, another legend in the field. My brother, Billy. I miss him, and I always get excited when I get a possible "sign" that he is still around.

DAVE WOULD LIKE TO THANK THE FOLLOWING: My amazing family, starting with Jim and Teri, my parents, for supporting me with love and respect, and my aunt Judi for inspiring me. My kids for understanding how busy Daddy can be. I love them all: Clifford, Keila, Nathan, Linus, Paci, and Ripley. Steve Versnick for seeing the potential and bringing our radio show to KTLK. Tim Dennis for bringing me back to radio and being my friend, cohost, and producer. Marley Gibson and Patrick Burns for including me in this project and keeping the dream alive.

CONTENTS

INTRODUCTION TO GHOST HUNTING

From our collective observations, it seems that belief in ghosts could be classified as the new black, and because of that, ghost hunting is the coolest thing since Guitar Hero, Prada backpacks, and the iPod.

Who are we and why should you listen to us?

Because we told you to! LOL! Okay, that doesn't really cut it, does it? The thing is, the three of us come from diverse and varying backgrounds and from different regions of the country, but one thing we share is an interest in the paranormal. Through our experiences in our own investigations, we feel that we can give you the best advice there is on how to get started in ghost hunting, safely, securely, and soundly.

First off, it's important to remember that there aren't any authorities in this field; no one is a paranormal expert. There are a multitude of paranormal investigators with differing philosophies on how to investigate. No one can truly say that his or her methods are better than anyone else's. Not even we can.

Each of the three of us holds a lifelong interest in the unexplained. With the explosion of interest in the paranormal within the last few years, we recognize that it is important for new investigators, such as you, to get started on the right foot. This work is a collaboration but should never be thought of as the final word.

Ghost hunting can be an exciting field to get into, although we must stress that more often than not, it's tedious, routine, and boring to the average person. Moreover, with the exception of a very small number of people who write books, work in television, or operate haunted-tour companies, ghost hunting is pretty much just a hobby for most people. Paranormal investigation is a true labor of love and a personal journey for attempting to understand the unexplained. Nothing more, nothing less. It's not something that one seeks out as a vocation.

And don't even think about ghost hunting as a profitable enterprise. It is pretty much universally frowned upon within the paranormal community to charge for conducting an investigation, and doing so virtually guarantees that you will be shunned by the rest of your peers in the field. Why is it considered taboo to charge? Because there is no way to prove the existence of ghosts and hauntings. Yep—you heard that right. *You cannot scientifically prove ghosts exist*—no matter how awesome a photograph you took. It's always open to other interpretations in the eyes of the scientist. As such, you can never conclusively tell a client his or her property is or isn't haunted. The best we can do is to confirm the unexplained activity within a location. Don't let this discourage you, though—we're not saying that these paranormal events don't happen. There is, in our opinion, strong evidence to suggest that they do. But if your goal is to find the final, irrefutable proof of the existence of ghosts and win over the rest of the world, you're bound to be disappointed.

As you start doing your own investigations, you'll no doubt come up with your own techniques and methods that will work uniquely well for you. We encourage you to develop your own distinctive style. Some investigators will approach ghost hunting from a more scientific perspective, while others will prefer a more esoteric or metaphysical approach. It's up to you to figure out what works best for you and your group. Just strive to always show respect to all you encounter in your investigations—that goes not only for the ghosts you come across but for living people too.

The most important piece of equipment there is to bring on a paranormal investigation isn't the fanciest electromagnetic field detector or the most expensive, top-of-the-line camcorder you can buy. It's a simple one: an open, objective mind. There have been many promising investigators (and even a few seasoned veterans) who get themselves swept up in the thrill of the hunt. No foul on their part—the adrenaline rush we experience while poking around a historic building in the middle of the night or being on a battlefield where thousands of soldiers lost their lives can and does distort our perception of reality. Being eager to find that incredible photograph or mysterious voice on an audio recorder, we become ripe for letting critical objectivity take a back seat. This is why re-reviewing your evidence the following day (or as soon as possible), after the adrenaline rush has worn off, is vital.

Remember that the best ghost hunters instill a healthy dose of skepticism in their investigations. And by skepticism, we don't mean disbelief. Rather, you need to investigate all possibilities of a "haunting" systematically and thoroughly before drawing an educated conclusion. Being open-minded allows you to examine all the facts and data for any logical reason that might explain a haunting. Belief in ghosts and spirits is fine as long as you don't allow it to weaken your perception and investigations. It's a fact that most ghost hunters *do* believe in ghosts, but it's definitely not a prerequisite to being a ghost hunter.

Before you start investigating, you'll need to know some basic things about ghost hunting and learn some tools of the trade, which we'll discuss throughout the book. Most of the things we'll be touching on you've probably seen on the many paranormal televisions shows that are out there. While you might glean some good ideas from these shows, you should not use them as an absolute training guide. This might seem odd coming from three people who have all been featured on these types of shows, but the truth is, TV can distort reality. Some shows have been known to portray ghost hunters in a less-than-favorable light or using questionable techniques to find ghosts. A few have even presented evidence and had its validity questioned by some. We want to see that the next generation of ghost hunters gets started on the right foot.

Why in the world would you want to hunt for ghosts?

No one really knows what ghosts are, because no one has ever come up with indisputable proof that they exist. For as long as we can remember, there have been ghost stories. The Bible mentions ghosts left and right. Ghost stories were passed down through the centuries within families and organizations as part of the fabric of life. People have written about ghosts, they're in the movies, and now, with all the shows on the air, they're part of the mainstream media.

Did you know that according to a Gallup Poll, roughly one-third of American adults believe in ghosts? Only 7 percent of Americans surveyed said they *don't* believe in some form of the paranormal (UFOs, ghosts, Bigfoot, etc.). And you can bet there are a lot of people who have had ghostly experiences who may not have ever shared their stories out of fear that their friends would poke fun at them. We seem to be in a new era of "enlightenment," however, in which people like to share their stories and seek out people with similar experiences.

But why would you want to *hunt* for ghosts?

There are many reasons. Most investigators get started in this hobby to fulfill their own personal curiosity. Perhaps it's that never-ending quest to solve one of the world's great mysteries—what happens after we die—that keeps people like us investigating haunted locations. Can we possibly make contact with our loved ones after they have passed on? Other investigators see it as a sort of "call to duty," such as wanting to help "trapped" spirits cross over. Others have a techie mindset and enjoy testing out scientific equipment. Then, of course, there is the thrill factor of the hunt. The reasons vary, but in the end the thing that matters is why *you* want to chase after ghosts.

You might want to approach your investigations like any good TV cop would, always looking for clues and explanations to help "crack" the case. You always need to be aware of all logical reasoning for why reported sightings or incidents occur. You want to thoroughly go over an investigative site with a fine-tooth comb, looking for any clue to help explain the paranormal happening. As you begin investigating, you'll develop your own habits and patterns that work for you and your group, and you'll likely discard those techniques that don't work for you. Hopefully you won't discard this book altogether.

No matter why you go ghost hunting, whether it be for spiritual reasons or for the thrill factor, you always need to be clear-headed, rational, and looking for explanations for anything you or your team experience. Good ghost hunters tell it like it is and reveal the truth, even if the "ghost" on the video turns out to be a plastic bag blowing in the wind. It seems everyone and his or her mom knows a few "ghost hunters" these days, not all of them taking a good, rational approach to investigating or representing the field in a positive way.

Who can go ghost hunting?

"I've never seen a ghost. I've never heard a spirit. I've never experienced anything paranormal. Can I still go ghost hunting?"

No. Absolutely not. Put this book down immediately and slowly back away. *Kidding!* Of course you can go ghost hunting! You don't need a fancy college degree. You don't need thousands of dollars in equipment either. The three of us have been active in our ghost hunting for years: a writer, a techie/TV personality, and a radio-show host. We each began researching, reading, investigating, and developing our techniques back when we were in our teens. If we can do it, anyone can. Even you!

Many people start ghost hunting with the hope of seeing a ghost, and who can blame them? Those of us who have actually had such an encounter will tell you it is an amazing—and yes, sometimes frightening—experience. However, the reality is that actually *seeing* a ghost isn't all that common. Many investigators who have been doing paranormal research for years claim they have yet to actually see Casper. So if you're expecting to *see* a ghost with your own eyes, you may have to lower your expectations, as it may or may not happen for you. However, once you get immersed in this field, you're very likely to start having ghostly experiences involving smells, sounds, temperature changes, shifts in energies, etc. . . . and yet still you may never actually see a ghost. As stated before, you just need to go into all of this with an open mind and without any preconceived notions.

In this guide, we'll show you how to properly investigate any (allegedly) haunted locations through the use of equipment, scientific evidence, your five senses, and your common sense. We'll talk about the many gadgets out there available to aid in investigations. We'll also discuss working with psychics and mediums and how they can help justify other data you gather. We'll show you how you can set up your own investigative team and where you can go on your ghost hunts. There are many practical dos and don'ts associated with ghost hunting, and we'll touch on those as well. In general, we'll walk you through every stage of preparation to get you and your friends out for some serious investigating.

One thing that's very important to emphasize is that this is a *hobby*—not a profession. We each see a steady stream of e-mails from young people asking how much money they can expect to make if they choose to become "professional" ghost hunters. The real question should be "How much can I expect to *spend* to become a ghost hunter?" There is equipment to purchase. There is gas to pay for when driving to and from locations, and in some instances there are hotel accommodations to cover for if it's an overnight road trip. As with any other hobby, there are certain expenses involved.

And just as in any other hobby, you get out of ghost hunting only what you put into it. If you arm yourself with the appropriate equipment, gather the strongest team of investigators, and act in a professional manner, the more success you'll have. Remember also that *you* are one of the most important tools in the investigation. A rational mind outweighs all the ghost hunting gadgets in the world.

As you can see, there is much more to being a paranormal investigator than watching a few TV shows and taking a slew of photos with a digital camera. It's hard work. But to the dedicated and enlightened investigator, it can be a true spiritual awakening to find evidence that death may not be the end for us, but a new beginning.

We hope that the tidbits we pass along in this book are helpful to you and your team and get you well on your way to successful ghost hunting. The world is full of interesting places and many mysteries. How amazing it is to research those things that are beyond our current understanding! It would be phenomenal if you could take all that we teach you and somehow be one of the first people to get actual concrete documentation of the existence of ghosts. If you should be that lucky person, please remember us when you accept the Nobel Prize!

Here's hoping you collect the greatest evidence of a haunting ever documented!

Casper and friends: What exactly are ghosts?

So…what exactly *are* ghosts? We've all probably cut eyeholes out of sheet and worn it around on Halloween or another occasion to spook someone. We've seen movies that deal with hauntings and ghosts and spirits—too many to even name. We've all been to a seasonal haunted house or a carnival fun house aimed at scaring us. We may even remember the old cartoon *Casper the Friendly Ghost* with his kind heart and willingness to help others. But there's so much more to what we perceive to be an actual ghost.

The word *ghost* comes from the Middle English word *gost* and the Old English word *gast,* meaning "breath/spirit," and has many other related forms in other Germanic languages. Dictionary.com defines *ghost* like so:

> **ghost** *(noun)*
> 1. The spirit of a dead person, especially one believed to appear in bodily likeness to living persons or to haunt former habitats.
> 2. The center of spiritual life; the soul.
> 3. A demon or spirit.
> 4. A returning or haunting memory or image.

It's easy to come up with a verbal definition of what a ghost is . . . it's just words. But to pinpoint and define the reality of a ghost is a whole other ball of wax. How do you know *what* exactly is or isn't a ghost, spirit, or entity? Can you truly trust your eyes if you see an apparition? Are your glasses dirty, or is your imagination running wild? Are you experiencing a cold spot in a room? Is it a poorly aimed air-conditioner vent, or is it exactly the location where Uncle Fred used to sit and watch NFL on Sundays? What if you see an odd flicker of light? Did your parents not pay the power bill? Is something running out of batteries? Or is it some sort of atmospheric or environmental situation that you're witnessing? As a paranormal investigator, you have to constantly question things, events, and conditions around you, as well as what you're seeing, feeling, and hearing.

People have been reporting ghostly encounters as far back as anyone can remember—literally since the dawn of time. Every major world religion is based in some sort of spiritualism and belief in an afterlife. The Bible is chock-full of references to spirits and ghosts. However, there remains no definitive, indisputable, scientific evidence of ghosts and spirits. That is where teams of paranormal investigators come in handy. Through a dedication to discovery and a focus on the science end of things, teams throughout the world strive to investigate locations and capture the best evidence they possibly can in order to justify the existence of an afterlife.

In the next chapter, we'll discuss more in detail what we believe a ghost is and even go into the different *types* of ghosts! Bet you didn't know there was more than one, did you?

History of the Spiritualist movement

THE FOX SISTERS. FROM LEFT TO RIGHT: MARGARET, KATE, AND LEAH

We can't exactly determine the absolute first time people began attempting to seek out and communicate with spirits. However, many people trace the beginning of modern-day ghost hunting back to the so-called Spiritualist movement, which started around 1849 with the Fox sisters. There are many books that cover the entire topic of this, so we'll keep it simple just to fill you in.

Adolescents Margaret and Kate Fox claimed to have mediumlike powers that enabled them to speak to the dead. With their oldest sister, Leah, as their manager, they toured all over the country to many cities, hosting séances that featured moving objects, knocking noises, and levitating tables. The public was enthralled with them and the apparent door they'd opened to another world. Many people accused them of being fakes and frauds, but it didn't keep the crowds away. Their popularity lasted until around 1885, when the interest in Spiritualism declined and the rise of skepticism increased. The whole Spiritualist movement pretty much came to an end in the 1920s.

Tomfoolery with photography

From the onset of photography in the mid-1800s, a handful of photographers figured out that they could create what is known as a *double exposure* by taking the film plate and exposing it twice. At the time, very few photographers, let alone common people off the street, fully understood how images were recorded onto film. A few less-than-honest photographers realized that through use of the double exposure technique, they could create photographs that appeared to contain ghostly apparitions.

William H. Mumler was one of the most successful at this. He would prey on grieving family members who had recently lost a loved one by charging them to come in for a sitting and with the promise of making contact with the departed, provide photographic "proof" that their deceased was still with them.

Mumler's technique was simple. With his camera set on a tripod, he would have the primary subject, who had paid for the session, sit in a chair in the studio and would proceed to expose several photographic plates of the subject. After the subject had left, with the chair still in place, Mumler would have a second subject (often a local actor or actress with whom he was friends) stand behind the chair, usually looking in the direction in which the first subject was sitting, sometimes seeming to embrace him or her. When the photographic plates were later processed, the grieving family members were elated and relieved to find "evidence" that their loved one was still present. Of course, the second ghostly subject in the images sel-

MUMLER'S SELF-PORTRAIT,
APPARENTLY FEATURING
THE GHOST OF HIS COUSIN,
WHICH BEGAN HIS CAREER.

HOUDINI WITH LINCOLN
SUPERIMPOSED.

dom resembled the person who had passed on. Mumler explained that we didn't always look the same in the afterlife as we had in life. As he was the "expert" on these techniques, few questioned his authority or explanations. Eventually an undercover reporter from the New York newspaper the *World* revealed the secret double-exposure technique and figured out that Mumler was up to no good. After that, Mumler's career had many ups and downs until he died in poverty in 1884.

While most people recognize Harry Houdini as possibly the greatest escape artist and stage magician of all time, he was also known the world over as a skeptic and investigator of spiritualists and mediums. He went to great lengths to expose frauds that had managed to fool scientists and academicians alike. He would even go so far as attending séances in disguise, having a police officer and reporter with him ready to help him reveal the situation. He debunked many a spiritualist who preyed upon people's sadness, loss, and weakness.

All the fraud and deception linked to the Spiritualist movement has given the investigation of the paranormal a black eye that we're still feeling today. But through the work and dedication of the thousands of paranormal groups working out there now, we're doing our best to make up for the misdeeds of the past.

Look at all the TV shows!

You can't scroll through the television guide without running up against a paranormal television show, special, feature, or documentary. They're everywhere: shows that feature haunted locations, teams of investigators, psychics and mediums, scary situations, people in need of help, etc. All of these shows demonstrate many ways of approaching a paranormal investigation. Many attempt to educate people as to the tools and science available. Most important, these shows are a unique opportunity to reach out to the next generation of ghost hunters.

However, you must keep in mind that so much of our work in this field is distorted by the very eyes and ears we experience it through. What we see and what we are told is often skewed by the mass media that delivers it to us. While we are all entertained watching ghost-hunting programs and paranormal investigations on television, it's important to remember that it's just that: entertainment. We urge the new generation of would-be ghost hunters to take media accounts of paranormal activity with a grain of salt. No investigation takes place in thirty minutes. What you see on television is almost always altered in the editing room. Editing allows for compression of time and for tossing out the lion's share of moments on investigations when nothing happens. No, you're not going to experience a paranormal event on every investigation. The harsh reality is that 99 percent of the time on an investigation is spent waiting for something to occur, if it occurs at all.

Nor should it be construed that what is presented on television is the final, irrefutable word. We are all still learning in a field that is almost entirely hypothetical in nature. Investigators on television can (and do) make mistakes in assessing the evidence they collect. As such, paranormal evidence is always inconclusive. Reread that last statement a few times until it soaks in, because we feel it's very important to keep that mindset if you want to be a good ghost hunter. At present, there is no "smoking gun" pointing the way toward the existence of paranormal phenomena. Data collected currently cannot withstand the scrutiny of science. So we are left to speculate and hypothesize on the phenomena we observe and document. While it's fun to entertain the notion of the existence of ghosts, it's still questionable at the end of every investigation. So you're investigating phenomena that may or may not be caused by ghosts. In fact, most of the time these phenomena have lame, mundane, normal explanations. That creaking door that opens on its own needs some oil and a handyman to adjust the jamb. That mysterious knocking behind the wall is a loose hot-water pipe that needs to be tied down. And that horrid, demonic screeching in the middle of the night is really the neighbor's cat getting into a fight with her "boyfriend."

It's prudent to point out that just because a person or group appears on television does not automatically make them the best investigators out there. Among the best *known* perhaps, but not necessarily the best. Investigators make their names in the field based on their merits and contributions—not the number of autographs signed or minutes of airtime. So treat television programs for what they are intended to be—entertainment, and not a 100 percent accurate portrayal of paranormal investigation.

CHAPTER TWO
DIFFERENT TYPES OF HAUNTINGS

Before we describe the different types of hauntings, we also need to point out that most investigators of the paranormal differentiate between a *spirit* and a *ghost*—even though the terms are often used interchangeably.

When we die, it's believed by many that an essence of our state of being, sometimes called the *soul,* will "cross over" into another place or dimension. The religious among us might call this place in the afterlife heaven. Whatever you choose to call it, many believe that it is the true destination of our being when it passes out of this life into the next. And for most of us, that's exactly what happens. When someone successfully "crosses over to the other side," we might refer to that person as a "free spirit" that is no longer confined to this world alone. It's believed that the free spirit may come back to our plane of existence to visit its family and friends from time to time, especially in moments of crisis. There are also many reports of people on their deathbeds talking with deceased family members whom they claim to see, but who are visible to no one else in the room. These types of apparitions are typically referred to as *visiting spirits.* While they may be disturbing to some, most people find such visitations calming and reassuring that they one day will be reunited with their loved ones.

While becoming a free spirit appears to be the norm for the majority of people who have passed on, unfortunately for some, the process of crossing over may not always go as planned. For various reasons, it's believed that some get "stuck" halfway between our life and the next and become what is commonly referred to as a *ghost.* When a ghost of a departed individual occupies a particular location or attaches itself to a living person or even an inanimate, material object, we might say that location, person, or object is *haunted.*

So why might some people become ghosts and haunt people, locations, or objects? Well, aside from taking advantage of the irresistible opportunity to scare the living out of their wits, there are several ideas here.

One possible explanation says that some spirits consciously choose to stay behind in this world. Perhaps they feel they have unresolved problems from their former lives that need to be taken care of. In the 1990 hit movie *Ghost,* starring Patrick Swayze, Whoopi Goldberg, and Demi Moore, Swayze's character, Sam Wheat, resists crossing over at the moment of death once he realizes he has been murdered. Knowing that he might be the only one who can solve the mystery of his untimely death, he begins to assemble the pieces of the puzzle. This "unfinished business" is often cited as a key reason for a ghost to haunt a location or person.

Another reason it's believed spirits might not properly cross over is for fear of *divine retribution* or being judged. Maybe these individuals did not lead entirely pure lives, and they fear they will be punished for their past deeds if they should have to confront their god face to face. Instead of taking that risk and going for what's behind "door number two," they might choose the consolation prize and just remain in the familiar world that they once lived in.

A third reason, as strange as it might sound, is perhaps some don't even realize they *have* died. We know what you're thinking—how dense does someone have to be not to think "Duh—I'm looking down at my body, and I can float through the ceiling! Hmm . . . maybe I'm dead?" Well, in the instance of someone who dies under anesthesia on the operating table or while under the influence of alcohol or other drugs, that person might simply believe he or she is still heavily sedated and wander about in a sort of ethereal daze, unable to accept or comprehend the fact that he or she has died.

Another theory we have recently begun to consider is that it may be the living who keep the dead from crossing over. It is our need to cling to them, to keep them here, close to us, that keeps them from feeling they can move on. They sense that if they leave us, they may be disappointing us or letting us down. So, in effect, it may be our very grief and inability to let go that keeps spirits from moving on to their next level.

In the case of an inanimate object that is reported to be haunted, it might have been an item of great importance to that person while he or she was alive. We're all familiar with the tales of pirates allegedly haunting their buried treasure and "cursing" any who dare to disturb it. Then there are the instances of toys that are haunted. Perhaps a particular toy provided a sense of security for a child, and even in death he or she refuses to part with it.

And one more interesting concept as to why ghosts exist or don't appear to cross over borrows a page from the playbook of some Eastern religions. This theory says that when we pass on, we move on to the next level, be it heaven, nirvana, or just the next plane of existence. But only the best of who we are moves on: the purest parts of our being. In other words, we might truly have a "split personality" when we die—the "enlightened" parts of us separate and move on, but the rest stays behind: the primitive "animal" aspects of our souls. This might explain why a haunting usually consists of simple communications like banging, slamming, flickering of lights, and short verbal messages like "Hello" or "Help me." The spirits involved represent the raw instincts of their former beings, the territorial side, which may explain why ghosts congregate at locations like old prisons, hospitals, and mental wards. They are subject to the pack mentality that is played out in nature all the time—safety and comfort in numbers, staying with others that are like them. Think about it—if you had a choice when you died, would you want to hang around the ditch where your car went off the road, or would you rather go and eavesdrop on your favorite band or celebrities? Wouldn't you rather haunt the beaches in Hawaii instead of a hospital ER ward? Who in his or her right mind wants to stay in some creepy, boring place for all eternity? But what if all that is left behind is our base animal instinct that can't really think on its own or that doesn't have real emotions? It would make sense as to why some spirits continue to cling to certain places, people, or objects.

Any of these circumstances (or more) might be reasons for someone to become a ghost as opposed to crossing over and becoming a free spirit. It's generally considered that being a ghost, either because of happenstance or by choice, is a tormented existence. If some ghosts are self-aware, if these souls are truly trapped and confined to our world, they might be compared to caged wild animals. They survive, but not in their natural state of being, and they may be depressed, sad, or even angry that they are "trapped." Consider it—if you were "imprisoned" someplace and invisible, watching people pass by who for the most part were totally unaware that you were there or, if they could see or hear you, ran away from you . . . you'd probably be depressed as well.

Fortunately, we as ghost hunters might be able to help. Many of these entities may simply need guidance and reassurance to cross over. Many researchers believe that once the true nature of a ghost's condition is explained to the entity, it will not want to remain here. One method used to assist a ghost in crossing over is very simple: having a medium who can communicate directly with the ghost explain to it that it simply needs to think of and call out to its loved ones who passed on before (and/or after) it did. Many mediums report that the ghost will report seeing a bright light and its loved ones emerging from the light. When this happens, the medium then instructs the ghost to embrace its loved ones and return with them into the light. At that moment, communications will cease and activity associated with the haunting should stop or greatly diminish.

A medium may not be necessary, however. Experience shows that anyone might verbally communicate with a ghost. If you have established a two-way dialogue with a ghost using a device such as the K2 meter (see chapter five, "Equipment Used in Investigations," for more information), you might be able to guide the ghost over using a similar dialogue and technique as described above.

A VAPOROUS ANOMALY OR A
STINKY FART—YOU DECIDE.

Types of apparitions (assorted ghost flavors with a free prize in each box)

Vaporous anomalies

No—we're not talking about the stinky fart one of your team members just unleashed because he ate a bowl of refried beans three hours before the investigation. Ghost sightings are frequently reported as mists or vapors. These may be either directly observed with the naked eye or documented in still photos or video. One must be careful to rule out smoke as a possible cause. For this reason, it's very important to forbid anyone from smoking or burning incense in the area during an investigation. If it is unusually dusty in an area, dust kicked up from foot traffic and automobiles must be taken into consideration as well. Likewise, fog and especially exhaled breath during cold weather are often mistaken for vaporous anomalies.

FULL-BODIED APPARITIONS (FBAs)

The full-bodied apparition or FBA isn't a super-secret agency of the United States government. The FBA is exactly as its name implies—a ghost that appears to have a full body from head to toe. To see an FBA is a rare event (it's rarer still to document one on film or video), and many paranormal researchers admit that they have never directly observed an FBA. This is obviously considered the ultimate paranormal encounter. If you already have, or should ever encounter an FBA in the future, consider yourself incredibly lucky, since many of your peers in the field will never be as fortunate.

PARTIAL-BODIED APPARITIONS (PBAs)

Sometimes a ghost is seen with only a partial body, many times just a torso and head, with the legs cut off at the waist. And some PBAs have been seen as only a pair of disembodied legs walking! The ghost of a magician's assistant who was accidentally sawed in half? Hmm . . .

In an interesting example of a PBA sighting, one homeowner reported seeing a residual ghost from the waist up moving up a flight of stairs with the waist at step level. This odd ghostly appearance didn't make sense to the homeowner at first, but after doing additional research into the history of the house, it was learned that the staircase had been rebuilt and elevated up about two feet from where it had been before. The ghost was merely a *placed memory* or *residual energy* from the time when the staircase was at that lower height (more about residual or placed memory later in this chapter). And because the haunting reflected back to a time when the staircase was at this lower elevation, the apparition continued to appear as if the staircase were still two feet lower.

SHADOW PEOPLE

These anomalies have been reported for many years, but only recently have investigators begun to take note and classify them in their own category. *Shadow people* (also known as *shadow men, shadow folk, shadow beings,* or *dark entities*) are full- or partial-bodied apparitions that appear as dark, two-dimensional shadows. Some investigators find that shadow people appear as dark forms in one's peripheral vision and disintegrate or move between walls and doorways when noticed.

PHANTOM VEHICLES

Not all ghosts are necessarily spirits or memories of people or beings. Perhaps one of the most interesting classes of apparition sightings involves that of vehicles. There have been countless reported sightings of ghosts over the years taking on the form of vehicles. Phantom automobiles, airplanes, ships, and even trains have been sighted.

One of the most famous phantom vehicle sightings is that of President Abraham Lincoln's funeral train. When Lincoln died, thousands of people came out to pay their respects to the slain president. They met his funeral train as it slowly made its way through the countryside. The outpouring of grief from the people was unprecedented for any fallen president before or since. Much of the rail route the train took between Washington, D.C., and Springfield, Illinois, where he was laid to rest, no longer exists. However, it is said that on the anniversary of the train's journey to Springfield, an apparition of the funeral train can be observed silently steaming across the countryside, retracing the route it followed back in 1865.

Classes of hauntings (not a school for ghosts)

When people talk about a location being "haunted," we assume that means that the place is inhabited by ghosts of people who died at that location. But that may not always be the case.

Paranormal investigators generally classify hauntings into four different categories or types of hauntings.

INTELLIGENT HAUNTINGS

This is probably what most people think of when they hear the word "haunted." An intelligent haunting is defined as paranormal activity in a location that appears to be self-aware. That is, the energy is aware of its environment and those within it. The intelligent haunting may choose to interact with the living people in that area and deliberately make its presence known. A person with psychic abilities may communicate and converse with the spiritual being directly.

Note that while the ghost or ghosts associated with an intelligent haunting may be aware of their location and the living people within it, as was stated earlier, these entities may not always be aware that they have died.

RESIDUAL HAUNTINGS

Sometimes also known as "place memory," a residual haunt can best be described as a "recording" of an event in time that will "play back" when the conditions are right. Unlike intelligent hauntings, the residual haunt is not aware of its condition or environment. There is nothing to interact with here, any more than you could interact with the actors and actresses while watching a TV show or movie.

In our experience, the vast majority of hauntings appear to be consistent with a residual imprint of a past event. A hypothetical example of this might be when an occupant of a house has passed on. Every day for the last twenty years of his life, this person's daily routine concluded with coming home from work, opening and closing the front door of his house, and walking upstairs. After this person passes on, the new occupants of the house might report continuing to hear the front door open and close and footsteps walking upstairs. This person's day-to-day routine became so routine, it recorded a residual imprint in the location where he lived and spent much of his time.

Another reason a location might acquire a residual haunting is if a traumatic event occurred in that location. Untimely deaths—particularly violent murders and battles from past wars—are believed to create unusually strong residual imprints. The charged emotion of such a sudden and tragic passing may be so intense that the memory of that event becomes a permanent fixture of that location.

The apparition of Abraham Lincoln's funeral train that was described earlier would be one very good example of a residual haunt or place memory.

POLTERGEIST HAUNTINGS

Poltergeist is a German word that literally translates to "noisy ghost." Poltergeist activity or hauntings are defined by movement of physical objects by unseen forces. A door opening and closing on its own might

A NEWSPAPER REPORTER TOOK THIS PICTURE OF TINA RESCH CAUSING A TELEPHONE TO FLY ACROSS THE ROOM.

be one example of poltergeist activity. A glass being violently thrown across the room and shattering against the wall would be another example. Fortunately, such intense, violent outbursts are rare.

There are two schools of thought regarding poltergeist activity. One says that the physical manifestations are the work of ghosts or spirits. Obviously the lack of a physical body means that a spiritual entity would need to expend a tremendous amount of energy to move physical objects. This would explain in part why poltergeist activity is so rare.

However, there is another explanation that may be at work here, one that attributes such manifestations not to the work of ghosts but rather to the living.

It's believed by some, and there is a good deal of academic research to support this idea, that these physical manifestations might be caused by a living subject in the vicinity. Researchers refer to this subject as a human poltergeist agent or HAP (yeah, it seems like it should be HPA, but it really is known in the field of parapsychology as HAP—don't ask us why). As amazing as it sounds, the HAP is completely unaware that he or she is responsible for these manifestations and, in most cases, is just as frightened (or amused?) as other subjects witnessing the mysterious movement of objects by unseen forces!

The reasons for such activity are not entirely agreed upon by researchers, but one theory suggests that it might be caused by a hormonal imbalance. An overwhelming majority of poltergeist cases involve adolescent teenage girls. It's believed that raging hormones as the young female HAP begins or ends puberty may be the cause of such "psychic temper tantrums." In some unfortunate instances, the HAP has been the victim of abuse, which might further the intensity of the hormonal imbalance and involuntary outbursts of psychic energy, also known as *psi* (pronounced "sigh").

Perhaps the most famous instance of this has come to be called the Columbus Poltergeist Case, which occurred back in the mid 1980s. The HAP subject's name was Tina Resch. Tina's mysterious abilities were documented numerous times by academic researchers and even members of the press. Physical objects such as telephones and television remote controls would abruptly fly off the table near Tina and end up on the other side of the room.

As is the case with many HAPs, Tina's abilities began to diminish and eventually disappeared altogether as she ended puberty and began her adult life.

TRANSIENT HAUNTINGS
In most ghost hauntings, the entities are believed to be both earthbound (that is, trapped) *and* tied to a specific location. This might be a house they lived in while alive. There are also many well-known hauntings of theaters believed to be caused by the ghosts of performers who once graced those theaters' stages. In these cases, the passion felt by the people who lived or worked in these places might have been so strong in life that it binds them there—even in death.

Location-specific hauntings are believed to be the most common. However, there is another possibility, known as a transient haunting. Some researchers also refer to these as "drop-in" hauntings.

The transient haunt is an earthbound ghost but one that is not bound to a single location. This entity is able to roam almost anywhere on the earth's surface. Transient entities are believed to be responsible for many "on and off" or inconsistent hauntings. The entity might happen to be passing through an area and see something or someone that piques its interest. The transient might take residence at this location for a period of time ranging anywhere from minutes to several months before moving along.

CHAPTER THREE
PRACTICAL AND SENSIBLE DOS AND DON'TS WHILE INVESTIGATING

When taking your team out on an investigation, there are some practical and sensible dos and don'ts everyone in your group should adhere to. First, let's look at the dos.

Do . . . get permission to investigate the location that you are going to.

This is very important for several reasons. First, from a legal perspective. Being on privately owned property without permission is trespassing. It's illegal and could land your team in a jail cell with stiff fines. You can bet that your parents won't be pleased with your new hobby if they are getting a call from the local police department to come and bail you out of jail.

Next, from an ethical perspective. It makes *all* paranormal groups look bad if even one is caught trespassing. Your peers in the field will shun your team if you "close doors" for them to investigate locations because you got busted for trespassing. Not cool.

It's also important to have permission for your safety and the safety of everybody in the group. Most ghost hunters will tell you they have sneaked into places they shouldn't have and have encountered dangerous stuff like collapsing ceilings; broken or missing stairs; rotting, loose, or missing floorboards; and exposed electrical wires. Some have even encountered old asbestos insulation, which is a huge health threat if you are exposed to it. If you go to an active location without permission and you or a teammate get hurt, the owners may be forced to close the building permanently or perhaps tear it down, which will remove a great potential location from future investigations.

Aside from structural issues, some of these old abandoned buildings have become homes for drifters, gangs, and drug dealers. As most investigators will tell you, it's not the ghosts that frighten us, it's the living people you might encounter while investigating.

Getting permission can be as simple as making a call or sending an e-mail. Be patient, as sometimes there's a lot of red tape surrounding these locations. The chance to get permission and officially be invited to investigate can be very cool. If you don't know whom to contact, you can always start with city hall, as they'll know who holds the deeds on those properties that are of interest to you and your group. Local law-enforcement officials or members of the fire department are great resources to ask as well.

And speaking of law enforcement . . . if your group has no adult membership, why not approach a cop and ask him or her to be a mentor for your group? Police officers are trained to notice things we "normal" folks don't, and they may be helpful in an investigation. Many officers are already interested in the paranormal field and are willing to lend a helping hand. They may have better access to locations, and they also bring with them a level of authority when trying to secure a location for investigation. The most important reason to include a mentor on your team is for safety, and there's nothing better for that than having a cop to escort you on your investigations. Most all police officers are trained in basic first aid in case of emergencies. It'll also set your parents at ease knowing there is some adult supervision on these cases. And we all know that the happier Mom and Dad are, the easier things are for *you!* Besides, your group will be the coolest around if you can boast you have a cop on your team.

The bottom line here is, play it smart and get permission *first*—you're doing your group and other groups a huge disservice if you don't.

Do . . . know your surroundings.

Always start an investigation by looking over the location in the full light of day so that you know what you're going into and can avoid any harmful or dangerous things. This is when you should employ your most crucial tool for ghost hunting: a notepad. Write down anything and everything you see that can help your group later. Sketch a basic map (it doesn't need to be to scale) and make notes of things like these:

> There's a broken window (upper left pane) in the bedroom.
> There are floorboards missing in the back hallway.
> There is a seven-headed demon hiding in the basement.

This way, as you're investigating later and catch a cold breeze or hear mysterious voices coming from the basement, you can go back through your notes and confirm your findings from earlier. This is really good to help you remove any false positives, which are things that may appear to be paranormal at first glance but are really things that can be explained some other way. When you're doing your dry run is a great time to get base-level readings with your equipment too. Test for high levels of electromagnetic readings so that you can track the source while the location is well lit. Also, note the average temperature in the rooms in case you run across any drastic changes during your investigation later.

Don't limit the preinvestigation walk-through to just the inside of the location. Walk the perimeter of the areas and make notes of trees or bushes that touch or scrape windows, how far the place is set back from a road, whether headlights from the nearby road will be a factor in nighttime investigations, or if there are scents in the air. Ask questions of neighbors around the immediate area to get any insights into the neighborhood and the goings-on.

For example, you might set up a video camera to focus on the outside. However, if the neighbors have a motion-sensor light that is set to a high sensitivity and they let their dog out during your investigation, you may see lights going on and off. Those lights are likely to appear as anomalies on your video. If you know ahead of time that this is possible, it will help you as you are reviewing your evidence.

And during your investigation, make sure everyone on your team carries a good, powerful flashlight with fresh batteries. Even though you scouted a location during the day, things can and do look different under the cover of darkness. One brand of flashlight we highly recommend is the Maglite. Its line of heavy-duty flashlights can be purchased at nearly any store that has a good sporting-goods or camping section. They come in a variety of sizes and beam intensities, are extremely durable, and can withstand being dropped on concrete—though we don't encourage you to tempt fate by "stress-testing" your flashlight while on an investigation. Maglites are definitely more expensive than the flashlights you get at the dollar store, but they are built like a tank and will withstand many years of use and abuse. This is the brand of flashlight most often used by law enforcement for these very reasons.

Do . . . have an investigation partner.

Never ever ever investigate alone. Always have a teammate with you.

Why, you ask?

The answer is simple: safety should always come first. In case of injury or harm, there is always someone there to have your back.

Validation is another key reason to have a partner: if you experience something, you have somebody there who can validate that you've just experienced unexplained phenomena.

A partner or team will also keep you in check and assist you in a moment of panic. You may be a big, tough guy, but when you get into a haunted room and someone says, "Hey, in this room a frightening child-spirit with no eyes appears and is known to scream and try to rip out your eyes," and then you're left alone in this room, you begin twitching at every noise you hear and every breeze that touches your skin. If you've got somebody with you, it'll help keep you anchored and grounded so you're calmer and more relaxed. Remember, though, if panic sets in, get out of there. Always remove yourself from the investigation immediately to avoid a mass-hysteria situation, because if there's one thing worse than having one nervous Nellie in your group, it's having a whole group of twitchin', freaked-out nervous Nellies.

If you start to feel spooked or uneasy, take a couple of deep breaths and tell your partner. Then leave, if needed. This is another great time for you and your partner to pull out the notebooks and start jotting down observations and personal recollections. Now you know where you can focus the return investigation. Collecting this type of data without front-loading—which is defined as having prior knowledge about a case or an experience before the investigation begins—makes the evidence of personal experiences even stronger.

Do . . . wear comfortable clothing.

This advice goes out to both girls and guys. You may want to look great when you go out on a ghost hunt—especially if there are cute girls and/or guys involved—but take our word for it . . . the spirits won't be impressed. Glamming up is lost on the other side. Stick with comfort, not style. Wear something that's loose-fitting and comfortable to move around in. Sweatshirts and/or T-shirts with sweatpants are perfectly acceptable. Try to stay away from loud clothing, like corduroy that can scrape together or squeaky shoes. Avoid leather and slick windbreakers, as they will make reviewing your audio recordings for EVP a complete and total nightmare. You'll hear nothing but *swish, swish, swish,* every time someone moves.

A good suggestion is to wear team shirts or similar outfits. This way when reviewing photograph or video evidence, you can quickly identify team members and eliminate them as paranormal entities.

Do . . . stay hydrated and come rested and well fed.

Not to sound like the school nurse, but . . . take care of yourself physically before an investigation. Dehydration, hunger, and fatigue can cause stomach pains and growls, headaches, and dizziness, which also are attributed to paranormal activity. Seriously. Many times there have been reports of "I went into this room and got this buzzing headache," or "I got sick to my stomach and felt woozy." It may be there's no paranormal activity at all, but the fact that you haven't eaten, haven't slept well, or haven't had a drink of water can point to your symptoms. You can avoid false positives by following these simple suggestions:

• Make sure that you have water with you so that you can sip it throughout the investigation.

• Take a power nap before an investigation—all you really need is twenty minutes. You don't even have to fall sound asleep. Just lie down, relax, close out your mind, and you'll find yourself a lot more refreshed for your investigation.

• Eat a few light meals throughout the day and carry a candy bar, energy bar, or piece of fruit to stave off hunger.

• Avoid eating a heavy meal right before an investigation. The blood will go to your stomach to work on digestion, which can cause a sense of being tired. When the blood is diverted to your stomach, it robs it from the brain, which is needed for thinking, hearing, seeing, and smelling. Not even kidding. When you're full or you overeat, your senses are dulled. Once our hunger is satisfied, we no longer need the sense of smell to seek food, the sense of hearing to find prey, or the sense of vision to locate our target. Not meaning to get all prehistoric-caveman on you or anything, but it's true. This can be especially hurtful to ghost hunters, since we rely so much on our senses for investigations.

Do . . . experiment with your equipment and get to know how it works.

It's extremely important that you experiment with each piece of gear that you and your team members own before taking it on an investigation. Try taking photographs so you get to know what orbs caused by dust, moisture, insects, and other light anomalies look like. This way, when reviewing evidence at a later time, you can move quickly through and discard the false positives. Take a picture of Grandma's favorite chair, then have someone hit it and take another picture. Look at all the souls you have released back to heaven! Yay for you! Okay . . . maybe it was only dust.

Take photographs in different temperatures. Take them in the light of day, during sunset, at nighttime, and before sunrise. Notice how temperature and moisture changes in the air can cause orb activity to varying degrees.

Set up your audio recorders in spots throughout the location, and then talk in normal voices as you move throughout. In turn, talk in whispered tones so you can see how sensitive your microphones are and how much or little detail they can pick up.

Be sure to find out what footsteps sound like in shoes as well as barefoot.

Use your video camera and check its night-vision capabilities to determine if you need more external light sources. The night-vision illuminators that are built into most camcorders are effective only for distances of about ten feet. You might need to supplement the light with an external illuminator.

Notice how the night-vision and infrared (IR) light reflects and refracts on shiny objects. You'll see that anomalies will be caught on camera that your naked eye cannot see, and you will get a good understanding of how light is recorded on your video camera.

Understanding the working of your equipment and the effects normal things can have on it may be one of the most important steps in investigating. When making a purchase, don't be embarrassed to ask for help when picking out equipment. Just explain to the sales-clerks what you plan to use it for. They may have some of the best advice for capturing evidence, since they know the workings of the devices they're selling you.

Do . . . take extra batteries.

You're going to keep the Energizer Bunny in carrots for the rest of his life. Batteries are essential for any investigation, and you'd better have a bunch of extras. What for? Because the one thing paranormal investigators have learned consistently is that ghosts are battery-suckin' vampires. They just love to "drain" our batteries. This phenomenon is known as "power depletion" or simply "battery drain." It works like this: You might have a set of fresh, brand-new batteries in your flashlight. Everything is going fine, and then five minutes into your investigation, your batteries are mysteriously "dead." Not just flashlights—cam-eras, laptop computers, digital voice recorders, camcorders . . . anything that is powered by batteries is ripe for power depletion. This is considered a paranormal phenomenon in and of itself, so be sure to make mention of the time and place it happens in your investigation notes. It appears that the spirit entities draw off only products that are on, so if you have a recorder or camera on constantly, it's an easy conduit for them to plug into. At least that's the theory, and we're sticking to it.

Also, don't just toss your disposable batteries out because they got drained on an inves-tigation. Many times when removed from the location, they will be restored to their normal levels later on. Try testing them out on the drive back home—you might be amazed to find that they are "good as new" again. Pretty spooky, huh?

And now for the don'ts during an investigation:

Don't . . . drink alcohol or take drugs!

Just don't do it. It's not a good idea. Why? Again, this is where common sense comes into play. First off, it's illegal. Not trying to come across like Mom or Dad here, but if you're underage and drinking or smoking, or if you're doing illegal drugs, and the cops show up, you've got very good reason to be scared—and not because of the ghosts! Trust us—a writeup in the police blotter of the local paper is *not* the sort of "press" you want for you and your group.

Legalities aside, if your mind is in an altered state, your perceptions of reality will be affected. You have to be responsible about going into locations and people's homes. If you're under the influence and trying to conduct an objective investigation, your credibility as an investigator just got flushed down the toilet. Don't expect referrals or references from that homeowner. In these investigations, you've been called in to help. Be a professional about it.

But there is another concern that needs to be addressed. The other possible dangers of drug and alcohol abuse in the paranormal field are that you might open yourself up for negative attachments. Entities can cling to you and try to influence you in a very negative way. Nobody wants that. Drugs and alcohol remove or lower your natural protection and inhibitions and allow for the possibility of bad things to happen. Avoid them at all costs on an investigation.

Don't . . . wear reflective or glow-in-the-dark clothing.

Recently, during an investigation of Waverly Hills Sanatorium in Louisville, Kentucky— considered one of the top ten most haunted locations in the world—a picture was taken that would chill one's bones. At the end of a long, dark hallway stood a perfectly formed, black-silhouetted shadow person. It's creepy. No detail, just this jet-black image with this white swirling vortex in the middle of its chest.

Wow—this was a great piece of evidence.

Then about a week later, we were going through MySpace and found some photos of the people who attended the Waverly Hills event. Sure enough, one of the investigators was standing there in black jeans and a black T-shirt with a white tie-dyed spiral pattern in the middle. The light from the flash was just bright enough to catch the pattern and reflect off the shirt. Since the rest of the place was so dark and the camera was far away, a lot of the details were lost. So, this creepy spirit–shadow guy was nothing more than some dude at the event wearing the wrong shirt.

Another reason to avoid reflective clothing is that most people have no real idea how to work your cameras properly. We're not trying to bag on you and your friends . . . It's just a fact. Everybody likes to think he or she knows how to use the camera's settings, but most people don't. A lot of times on investigations, you'll take a picture and it'll go *flash, flash, flash, flash, POW* . . . doing the red-eye-reduction function. The red-eye reduction sends out a pulse of light, opening up the iris of the camera—the aperture. So now let's say someone goes walking across the hallway with reflective clothing on while you're taking that picture. You get an image of a white swirling mass running across the room. But in truth it was just somebody out of your view who walked past quickly and had reflective clothing on. That is how you end up with a really good piece of junk evidence.

Don't . . . wear shiny jewelry, watches, dangly earrings, necklaces, pins, brooches, or decorative rings.

We can all appreciate some well-worn bling, but leave it at home during an investigation. The reasoning behind this is that night-vision and IR light reflect and refract like crazy. IR light is infrared light and is used in night-vision for a lot of the different technologies out there. Instead of ghostly apparitions, you are more likely going to see reflections and refractions that you can't see with your bare eye that are taking place in a room, such as reflections of your watch face, jewelry, or glasses.

There was an investigation once in which one of the ladies attending had these long, dangly earrings with little spangles on them. She walked up behind the video camera, tilted her head to look down the hall, and then she walked by. Well, the IR light was illuminating the room from the back. As she walked past the camera, the light caught the reflection on her earrings, so it suddenly looked as if Tinker Bell sneezed, followed by this light pattern flickering across the screen. It wasn't until later, while reviewing video footage in which the woman showed up in another scene and turned her head, that the flicker of her earrings was noticeable. The light pattern was the exact same thing we'd seen before, so we realized our light anomaly had been debunked. So take off your reflective surfaces; it will just make for a better investigation and eliminate false-positive evidence.

Don't . . . wear shoes with hard soles or heels.

Avoid high heels, heavy boots, and for the love of God . . . please *do not* wear flip-flops on an investigation. You may look great, but the footwear styles mentioned are the number-one culprit for creating disturbances during audio-recording sessions. No one wants to hear the *clip-clop, clip-clop* of high heels or the *fwah-taka, fwah-taka* of your flip-flops during an evidence review—or at the investigation, for that matter.

Avoiding boots is important too for the reason that many haunting sounds include the sounds of boots from soldiers, the master of the house, etc. So if you are all wearing soft-soled shoes or socks and you pick up distinct boot steps on audio, you can immediately rule out investigator contamination. Maybe get a comfy pair of slippers that make no sound when walking. That way if you are investigating all night, you'll be comfortable and not a threat to the evidence collection.

Don't . . . wear perfume or cologne
while you're investigating.

One of the most widely reported styles of haunting is olfactory, which means you smell Grandma's perfume, Uncle Ed's pipe tobacco, etc. If you are coming to an investigation reeking of cologne or perfume, it can leave trace or residual scents in locations you have been. Anybody who's walked into a bathroom after someone else knows that sometimes . . . smells linger.

You also want to make sure you are clean and showered; just try to use unscented soaps and deodorant. No one wants to smell your funk. We're already considered geeks for being into ghost hunting, so don't be known as a smelly geek on top of it.

Don't . . . have your cell phone on. Better yet, don't bring it.

Turn off or leave your cell phone out in the car or in your bag, or don't bring it with you at all. Cell phones and PDAs let off some level of electromagnetic frequency leakage. It can actually affect a lot of the different equipment. The K2 meter is a perfect example. If you are standing there holding the meter switch down and somebody calls your cell phone, the K2 will react seconds before the phone rings, because it's picking up the radio frequency. It picks up the ring that's being sent into the phone. If you've got your phone in your pocket with the ringer and vibrate mode turned off and you're investigating using the K2 meter, if the meter starts lighting up, you're going to think you're getting ghost activity. But it's really just a call coming through. If you must bring your phone with you, make sure it's *really* off—many phones have a "standby" mode to conserve battery power but still transmit a signal intermittently. Make sure it's not merely on standby when you think it's switched off.

Another prime example of how our equipment can be influenced came while investigating a beautiful antebellum mansion in Atlanta, Georgia. There was one room in the house that has had reports of hauntings. In this room is a trunk that was sent there by one of the family members upon his return from the Civil War. Apparently, the trunk arrived home, but the soldier didn't because he was killed in an accident while returning from the war. However, the trunk is said to have the spirit of the soldier attached to it, and many investigative groups get crazy EMF readings in and around this trunk. As we investigated it, we had a guy standing in the room with an EMF detector. Every time he bent down closer to the box, the meter started spiking with all kinds of lights and sounds. As he stood up, everything stopped. So, are we to believe that the ghost was curled up in a fetal position inside the trunk? It was also observed that every time this investigator bent down, he brought his hand closer to his waist where he had a BlackBerry sitting on his hip. He was asked to take off the BlackBerry, which he did, setting in on a nearby table. When he did another EMF sweep of the trunk, mysteriously the ghost in the box had vanished. We had just removed a false positive from our investigation.

Don't . . . rely solely on your equipment, divination tools, or the word of a sensitive.

Your own equipment, divination tools, and sensitives are all effective methods of evidence gathering. However, the downside is that many investigators don't bother to look past the two-by-three-inch video screen, the set of divining rods, or the word of the sensitive. Technology is great, but you should get information from as many sources as possible, including your own eyes and ears. Personal accounts can be extremely effective if you have one team member be the video documentarian so the rest of the team can focus on cold spots, smells, sounds, etc. Then the videographer can come to the location where something appears to be happening and try to document it while it occurs. This way you get the personal account as it happens and use visual or audio technology for confirmation of the occurrence.

On the other hand, relying too much on subjective accounts is to be avoided as well. Too many times, a team that employs a sensitive will end up following the individual around, hanging on his or her every word and forgoing any type of formal investigation. Even the most accurate sensitives are not right 100 percent of the time. Let's face it, they are exciting and tell us a story and share a view on something we cannot experience ourselves, but their skills should be looked at as nothing more than one tool in what should be an arsenal.

Don't . . . use Ouija boards, automatic writing, or energy transference during an investigation.

The use of Ouija boards and such tools and allowing or inviting spirits to use you as a conduit can be a very risky and dangerous proposal. There are psychics and sensitives out there with years and years of experience who refuse to allow spirits that kind of control. Unless you really understand and know how to protect yourself spiritually and psychically, you should avoid this type of investigation. Allowing spirits to manipulate you by any means is opening a door to that world. That is when negative things can attach themselves to you and create a greater danger to you and to your client.

We will cover more of this in chapter nine, "Safe Hex: Protection for You and Your Team."

CHAPTER FOUR
GEEK TIME: TECHNOLOGY TALK

Okay . . . it's hard to have a chapter called "Technology Talk" without getting a little deep and, well, technical on you. This chapter is a bit deeper than the others. Just roll with it. It's important stuff.

Since the dawn of the electronic age, many people have claimed to receive communications directly from the spirit world through various electronic devices. An amateur radio operator in Great Britain once believed he heard the "SOS" distress call sent from the RMS *Titanic* as it was sinking. The problem was, he received this transmission in 1926—a full fourteen years after the doomed ship had gone down!

As technology has moved forward, technically minded paranormal investigators have done the same, constantly thinking up new ways to make use of the current technology in their investigations. The great American inventor Thomas Edison, who was responsible for many important inventions, including the electric light bulb and phonograph, believed that in time it would be possible to create a device that would allow communication with the spirit world. Edison once said the following in an interview:

> If our personality survives, then it is strictly logical and scientific to assume that it retains memory, intellect, and other faculties and knowledge that we acquire on this earth. Therefore, if personality exists after what we call death, it's reasonable to conclude that those who leave this earth would like to communicate with those they have left here. . . . I am inclined to believe that our personality hereafter will be able to affect matter. If this reasoning be correct, then, if we can evolve an instrument so delicate as to be affected, or moved, or manipulated . . . by our personality as it survives in the next life, such an instrument, when made available, ought to record something.

It's rumored that Edison was working on just such a device shortly before his own death, dubbed "the telephone to the dead." Edison never realized his otherworldly invention during his lifetime, but some have continued his work and even believe that they have received instructions on how to construct such a device from the spirit of Thomas Edison himself.

For those of you still awake, let's get into this a little further.

THE SPIRIT BOX . . . NOTHING TO DO WITH CHEERLEADING

A somewhat recent development in technical investigation of hauntings is a device known as the spirit box. And no, it's not used at pep rallies and football games to generate support for the team. It's a communication device that was invented by a man named Frank Sumption. People in the paranormal field have nicknamed this device "Frank's Box" in honor of its creator.

Sumption based the device's design on his experiments with an AM radio that is "swept" or rapidly tuned up and down the dial. Through all the gibberish, static, and noise on the airwaves, Sumption noticed something very peculiar happening: he would often get voices coming through in answer to questions he had asked. Through these communications, he believes he received additional instructions on how to improve this invention directly from the spirit world. Many paranormal investigators are continuing to research and contribute to the further development of the spirit box today.

On the lower end of the technology scale, any recording device may be used to capture electronic voice phenomena (EVP), or potential spirit voices. These are discussed at length in chapter seven.

POWER DEPLETION AND EQUIPMENT MALFUNCTION

In our investigations, we use a lot of equipment that runs off batteries and/or power cords. Many times we experience and measure activity on our various pieces of equipment in ways we did not anticipate. For example, batteries are notorious for becoming rapidly discharged in locations where paranormal activity is believed to occur. This phenomenon is known as power depletion, or as some investigators prefer to call it, battery drain. This is one of the most curious events—and the most common—that you may encounter during your own investigations. When power depletion occurs, the investigator may find that any battery-powered equipment (cameras, recorders, camcorders, laptops, or even flashlights) will suddenly and very abruptly have almost no power left within them. We've seen this happen with both brand-new, factory-fresh disposable batteries and fully powered rechargeable batteries. The spirits don't seem to have a preference. Power depletion typically occurs within five minutes of turning on the affected device. Even more curious is what may happen after the investigation. A device that had previously shown no power left on its battery may suddenly show battery levels restored to fully charged levels when the device is removed from the investigation location. This mysterious replenishment or recharging of the batteries seems to rule out defective or old batteries as being the cause of power depletion.

Another odd occurrence that may be experienced in active locations involves unexplained malfunctions by the various pieces of electronics. Many paranormal investigators note that the cameras and other equipment may unexpectedly turn off (or on) for no apparent reason. Computers seem to be particularly susceptible, and many of them demonstrate erratic behavior that is not reported at any other time. Such behavior seems to be related to and limited to the locations where investigations are being conducted.

So keep this in mind during an investigation: if your batteries suddenly show no power or your electronic devices start behaving unreliably, you may be experiencing paranormal activity.

TEMPERATURE ANOMALIES, OR, LIKE, WEIRD COLD SPOTS

One of the most frequently reported phenomena associated with alleged hauntings and ghosts is the so-called cold spot, or temperature anomaly. It is believed that when a spirit or ghost is present, it will "feed" off the heat energy in its immediate vicinity. Stripping the heat out of the air will, theoretically, cause the temperature to drop in that location. The plunging temperatures can be quite dramatic. Drops of ten to twenty degrees are typical, while more extreme fluctuations up to seventy degrees have been reported in very rare instances. These free-floating temperature anomalies are highly localized events, confined to a small area, usually only two or three feet in diameter. Cold spots are thought to happen on solid surfaces as well. It is believed that ghosts strip warmth away from walls and doors when they pass through them. Most of the time cold spots will be experienced for only a few seconds, but there are reports of these temperature anomalies lingering in a particular area for up to five minutes or more and experienced by many people. Far less common but also reported is the exact opposite—warm spots, where the temperature will actually increase in certain locations.

While cold and warm spots are frequently felt by paranormal investigators, it's a subjective or personal experience until it's recorded and documented on the equipment. To do this, the investigator will use a thermometer in his or her investigations. Not all thermometers are suited for documenting this type of event. Since a cold or warm spot usually lasts only a few seconds, the common glass thermometer that many people are familiar with is considered unsuitable for use due to its slow response time. In other words, the event will have come and gone before such a thermometer is able to measure it. You really need a digital thermometer that responds quickly enough to show that the temperature changed. Please see chapter five, "Equipment Used in Investigations," for more information on types of thermometers.

ELECTROMAGNETIC DISTURBANCES (IN THE FORCE)

Let's go back to science class for a moment—no groaning; this is important. As you may recall, the earth is surrounded by a naturally occurring magnetic field. This magnetic field, which is what causes a compass to point toward magnetic north, can be disrupted by other magnetic fields in the area. When this occurs such disruptions can be measured on a device known as an electromagnetic field (EMF) detector. It's believed that ghosts and spirits are composed of energy, and these energy fields may be able to disrupt the earth's magnetic field as well. If this is the case, we might be able to detect their presence with the aid of an EMF detector.

Since many man-made sources of EMF can disrupt the earth's magnetic field, the investigator must eliminate such sources as potential causes of an electromagnetic disturbance before it can be considered a possible paranormal event.

Using an EMF detector, the investigator will typically start his or her investigation by walking through a room and scanning the surfaces, also known as "sweeping" the location with the meter, making note of strong EMF sources behind walls, under floors, or in ceilings. Electrical appliances like television sets, computers, refrigerators, and air conditioners all are known to be responsible for creating strong electromagnetic fields. If possible, these appliances should be powered off during an investigation to eliminate false readings. Cell phones, BlackBerrys, and the like also give off a strong dose of electromagnetic energy and must be turned off during an investigation as well to eliminate the possibility of false readings.

SPIRIT PHOTOGRAPHY . . . AGAIN, NOTHING TO DO WITH CHEERLEADING

The most commonly collected evidence of alleged paranormal activity is in the form of photographs. Unfortunately, photography is an extremely complex subject, and there are numerous non-paranormal reasons why a strange anomaly might appear in a photograph. An entire book could be written about every photographic mistake that could be interpreted as a paranormal event. Let's briefly discuss some of the commoner mistakes made in photography during a paranormal investigation.

Perhaps the most widely documented and misinterpreted anomaly that appears in photographs is the infamous orb. These anomalies are so prevalent that we've dedicated an entire chapter to the understanding of orbs in the vast majority of photos. Please see chapter six, "What Are Orbs?"

Other common things incorrectly interpreted as signs of paranormal activity include obstructions in front of the lens. Strands of hair, a stray fingertip, a fingerprint smudge, even the camera strap have all been mistaken for evidence of ghosts.

Try taking various photographs while dangling these items in front of the lens to see firsthand and be able to identify such false readings when you encounter them during your investigations. For example, take a few strands of hair and hold them in front of the camera lens. Next, take a flash photo. If you've done this correctly, you'll see elongated "anomalies" that some investigators refer to as rods. Of course, the mysterious objects you just photographed are not paranormal in nature. However, it's important to recognize such errors when they occur in photographs in your investigations. A simple solution to this problem is to tuck long hair under a hat or pull it into a ponytail.

To prevent your fingertip from being the culprit, be mindful of how you hold your camera and where your fingers are placed at all times when snapping a photo. The infamous camera-strap anomaly can be eliminated by removing the strap altogether or making sure it is secured around your wrist or neck so that it will not partially obstruct the lens of the camera. These are no-brainer suggestions, but sometimes they're things we just don't think about in the heat of the moment of an investigation.

And finally, always be mindful of other light sources when taking photographs. Reflections within the camera lens are common when it is pointed in the direction of a bright source of light. These reflections can be the source of strange-looking anomalies in your photograph that might be mistakenly identified as evidence of the paranormal. Even the flash of your own camera reflecting off of a window or mirror can be responsible for photographs that seem to be paranormal in origin. Whenever you encounter a possible paranormal anomaly in your photographs, always try to recreate the situation. If possible, return to the location where the photo was taken under the same conditions that were present when you took the original, and see if you can't reproduce your results. If you can, you've eliminated that as a photograph of ghostly activity.

Are you still awake? Come on . . . it wasn't that bad. This is stuff you need to know that will be very helpful in your investigations. We've briefly touched on the application of a few forms of technology currently being utilized when ghost hunting. This is really only the tip of the iceberg. (Get it? Going back to the *Titanic* reference? Never mind.) There are many other aspects of technology that can be applied to paranormal investigations that have not been addressed here. Rely on your own curiosity to investigate, explore, and test other aspects of technology within your investigations.

However exciting and compelling technology may be in paranormal investigations, we've said it before and we'll say it again: the most important instrument of all is your open, objective mind. Always use your common sense and do not rely solely on what your instruments tell you.

34:20 - "no"

"My knees hurt - pain like a polio"

40:00 - Maureen start channeling
Something reaching out in
a nice way to Julia - which
temperature goes down

You have to rule everything out

43:56 - Something
45:15 - "yeah"
51:41 - "Chi"
53:57 - "sorry" ?

54:13 - So much warmer in museum

Snacking on Fritos

John Ward House   1:02:00

1:05:48 Something
1:07:34 Something

1:07:56 Maureen channeling
1:10:46 kept it hands in pocket
         so she wouldn't hit her

If you walk over a burial ground
of unmarked grave - you can channel
that person & get Shaolin house effect

1:12:15 Something

1:13:48 Mine & Jen's cameras died

         Candle broke

1:14:25 - something
1:18:04 - "bastard" (New England
                     Accent)
All #'s were to 55

1:22:58 - something

Jen had fever-feeling - like she's out
of her body

1:31:09 - something

Weaker part of your body - if you
have a weak part of a live wire,
the electricity will run through
there. Electricity runs to the
weakest point first. The body is
electrical - nervous system, so
your sensitivity is in the weakest
part

Channeling - you're not able to control
your thoughts. You don't feel like
you can think. Like something's
stopping you. Maybe Kendall
hears her channeling. Just fine if
Kendall doesn't want to channel -
but she does get a strong connection
Can understand her wanting people
to emulate it. But, it's important
to Kendall's development that she
try new things - can channel in
B&W when she's stronger & can do a
big finish type thing

Glass divination

DW_C0016   401 w/ Chris Fleming

0:30 blip
0:35 growl
0:47 - 0:58 - Whispering underneath
1:38 - 1:49 - Something underneath
5:27 - "no" ?
7:07 - something
8:04 - 8:18 - Something underneath
8:32 - Something when I'm hot
8:43 - Something when I'm hot
9:52 - Something
14:34 - click
14:41 - Something   (dowsing)
16:43 - "no"
18:54 - "yes"
20:00 - 20:09 - Something
20:39 - 20:46 - Noisy
23:56 - huffing
27:53 - Something
28:27 - Something

         418 w/ Chris

DW_A0021   Bottonwoods 4/5

1:00 - Something (energy)
1:04 - Something
1:09 - Something
4:12 - Julia going to faint   (Are there
       EMF going off   any spirits
       "Slow down"   here?)
Little girl is around us,
but is skittish - doesn't trust
Instant emotion got me.

       60 min of battery power dropped

15:08   Something

Something moving along in Mrs. Duncan's
room. Mrs. Duncan is skirting us,
but her energy is all around. EMF
going off

24:18 - Something
25:14 - blip

We scared her off w/ the light
Started coughing - whooping cough
"Easy, easy, easy."
"Leave."
"no"
"My legs won't move."

Up to attic -

Heart is slamming / lots of energy
Chasing ghosts w/ UV light
Lips & legs going numb

-30-

PAGES FROM MARLEY'S GHOST HUNTING JOURNAL

CHAPTER FIVE
EQUIPMENT USED IN INVESTIGATIONS

Every good ghost hunter should have a go-to kit of equipment to help out with all aspects of the investigation. This can range from the simplest items to some of the most high-tech gadgetry available. Each investigator has his own preference to what tools and equipment work best for him, and it's up to you and your team to decide what are the most effective items for your own investigations. Of course, one of the most important tools to use while investigating is you—your own common sense, as well as your own five senses. However, you can't always rely on your eyes, ears, and nose to detect paranormal activity. That's where all of the following equipment comes in handy for a ghost hunter like yourself:

NOTEBOOK AND PEN
It's vital to your research and evidence review that you keep good notes. Write down where you are, what the weather conditions are like, time, date, names of your team members, description of the location, etc.—anything that you think will be pertinent later when you all get together to go over the evidence and discuss the investigation. You may think you can remember everything, but trust us, you won't. Even the tiniest detail that seems important at the time it happens may slip your mind a day or two—or a week—later when you're going over your investigation. Keeping all your notes on each location/investigation in a notebook is a good way to organize your experiences and provides you with a way to go back and double-check anything, should you need to. Of course, carry pens and pencils with you so you'll have something to write with. You can also use your notebook to sketch out the location, showing electrical outlets and so on in order to see where you might be getting spikes of energy. (More on that later.)

FLASHLIGHT
Since ghost hunting is done most of the time in the darkness of the early-morning hours, it's sort of a no-brainer that you should carry a flashlight along with you. A lot

of times, you might want a smaller, clip-on flashlight to help you find equipment in the dark or make notes at a moment's notice. We recommend that you keep the flashlight off as much as you can so that your eyes can adjust to the darkness. However, in the case of walking up and down stairs or in areas where you could trip and fall, always light your way with a flashlight. This may sound obvious, but never shine it in anyone's face and keep it pointed to the ground when you are using it.

BATTERIES

Most of the equipment used in today's ghost investigations runs off of batteries, so it's essential that you keep a stash of batteries of all sizes (AA, AAA, 9-volt, D, etc.) handy in your ghost-hunting bag. In the odd instance that you and your team might be flying to a haunted location with your equipment, remember that your batteries cannot be loose; they must be in the equipment or sealed in a package. Ghosts and spirits love to suck the energy out of your equipment batteries, so bring extras so that you won't miss one second of evidence collection.

CAMERAS

As mentioned in more detail in chapter four, "Geek Time: Technology Talk," cameras are very important in our investigating. While digital cameras are easy to use, are convenient to carry around, and provide instant gratification in terms of allowing you to see your images right away, it's also smart to have a still camera on your investigations as well. There are benefits to both types of cameras. The thing about a still camera is it can produce higher-quality photographs, and you'll always have a negative to go along with it. Some investigators use specially modified digital cameras that can "see" infrared color. Infrared light is a portion of the electromagnetic spectrum beyond the red end of the rainbow and is invisible to the unaided human eye. Using an infrared camera, this hidden spectrum of light comes into view. Many interesting photographs that seem to contain ghostly apparitions have been captured in the infrared range of light.

VIDEO CAMERAS

Having a video camera to document the whole investigation while it's taking place is a good idea. These can be in the form of hand-held DVR cameras or full-size video equipment. Whatever you use, make sure you keep your tapes or disks properly labeled and catalogued to keep track of your location, time, and date.

DIGITAL VOICE RECORDER

In order to capture electronic voice phenomena (EVP) during your investigation, you need a digital voice recorder. You don't have to pay a fortune for one, as many of the best brands that seem to capture EVP are in the $30–$60 range. Brands like Sony, Panasonic, and Olympus are trusted names that have quality equipment for your EVP work. When using your digital recorder, make sure you record each team member's voice and know how it sounds so that if you encounter voices that don't match those, then you more than likely have disembodied voices showing up. It's also good to have a backup recorder in the event that you want to use them together or if one of them goes out.

THERMOMETER

Whether you're investigating inside or outdoors, it's a good idea to have a thermometer of some sort with you. Often you might encounter a cold spot. Almost all ghost hunters report running into cold spots during their investigations. Having a thermometer with you allows you to document the shift in temperature and back up personal experiences with scientific data. Probably the best thermometer to get is a non-contact thermal gauge, which allows you to point the thermometer at a particular area and grab that temperature. There are also thermometers that come with their own software that will record the temperature conditions in a room or location so that you can review them afterward to look for trends in the temperature.

There are two types of digital thermometers frequently used in paranormal investigations. One type known as a thermal spot meter or non-contact infrared thermometer. This one typically has a pistol-grip design. When you point the device at a place or object, the device will measure the surface temperature of that object. Research has shown that these types of thermometers cannot detect a free-floating temperature anomalies, as they are designed to sense the temperature of solid surfaces.

A second type of digital thermometer utilizes an electronic component known as a thermistor or thermocouple. These devices detect ambient or surrounding temperature of the air and are suitable for measuring a rapid temperature drop. With such a device, the investigator can either walk about the room or place the thermometer in a stationary location and observe the display, making note of any significant increases or decreases in the temperature. Note that breezes, drafts, or the output from an air-conditioning duct will cool all the air in a location, so be mindful of moving air currents where you are taking temperature readings.

EMF DETECTOR

If you watch any of the television programs out there about ghost hunting, you'll notice that everyone and his brother uses an EMF detector. An electromagnetic field detector or meter measures electromagnetic energies in a location. It can range in cost from $30 to as high as $400. The readout is usually a thin needle, an indicator light, or, most often, an audio beep. When using an EMF detector in a thought-to-be haunted location, it's best to do a "baseline" reading of the entire place to determine any "hot spots," like where power sources or electrical outlets may be. They are more likely that other areas to cause spikes in the meter readings. A house's wiring and appliances will also cause the meter to go off. (Just place an EMF detector near your clock radio.) Experiment with your meter, move it around, and don't be afraid to get it into cracks and crevices to check out readings. If you can't trace spikes on the meter back to anything electrical in the location, chances are you're dealing with something paranormal. Make note of any fluctuations throughout your investigation.

K2 METER

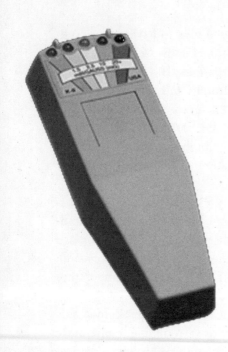

Recently, the K2 meter has become popular with ghost investigators because of its apparent ability to conduct two-way conversations with paranormal entities. The K2 is recognized by its string of yellow to green to red lights across the top of the meter. These lights measure the strength of the EMF the meter is picking up. However, investigators like psychic/medium Chris Fleming have had experiences in locations like the *Queen Mary* in Long Beach, California, and the Stanley Hotel in Estes Park, Colorado, where two-way communication was established in the form of yes/no questions, with the entity allegedly using the lights and their patterns to answer said questions.

COMPASS

A compass is a pretty cool thing for measuring simple magnetic and electromagnetic energy. It's usually small and doesn't cost a lot of money and is good to have in your tool kit. If there is any other force or energy field present, it will mess with the compass's sensitive needle. As you do with your EMF detector, you'll want to do a sweep of the location with the compass to make sure there are no magnets that would affect your readings.

LEVEL

This may sound a bit wack, but having a small level in your bag is a good thing in case you witness any kind of activity that may seem paranormal in nature but could be due to a crooked floor or shelf or a dip in a hallway, etc. If you have a level, you can place it in various locations and take pictures of the readings to prove that a surface is, indeed, straight.

NIGHT-VISION EQUIPMENT

If you have a little money to invest, you can get some cool night-vision goggles to help focus more in the pitch-black dark. Night-vision scopes can be purchased from around $150 on up into the thousands. The positive thing about such equipment is that it can allow you an ultra-clean look at the darkness. This certainly isn't a necessity, but it can be something fun to play with during your investigation.

HEADPHONES

A good set of headphones will help you listen back to any of the recordings you've made and give you a keener sense of what you're hearing. Any standard headphones will do. See if your digital recorder will allow you to listen at the same time you're recording. You may be able to hear the EVP as they happen.

MICROPHONE

An external mike on any of your equipment like your video camera or digital recorder can often help amplify sound and pick things up that the standard, built-in microphone might not be able to.

FARADAY BOX, CAGE, OR SHIELD

Named after its inventor, Michael Faraday, who created it in 1836, a Faraday box is made of conducting material like mesh and provides an enclosure that blocks out all other sound, static, and electrical fields. In the ghost-hunting community, it's thought that if you put a digital recorder in a Faraday cage and no other sound is allowed in, then any sounds you get recorded on it would have to be of a paranormal nature.

DOWSING RODS

When you think of *dowsing,* you may think of the Y-shaped stick out in the backyard that Grandpa might use to find a water source. In ghost hunting, dowsing rods made of metal are used to try to pick up on any electromagnetic energies in an area. It is thought that spirits may be manipulating the energy to move the dowsing rods in some particular way to bring about a particular result. This is similar to using a pendulum—a stone on the end of a string or chain that reacts to the earth's energies to provide yes/no answers. This is a form of divination and requires the user to "open himself" to energies that he might not be prepared for. We don't recommend using dowsing rods—or a pendulum—unless you have experience and training, as you could be inviting unfriendly elements to use you as a vessel for their entertainment.

COMMON SENSE

This could be the most important tool you use on an investigation. Understanding your equipment, how it works, what it is used for, and the basics of why it does what it does is important, but keeping a cool head and thinking through a situation can be even more helpful. You will find that in 95 percent of all situations that you encounter, there are logical explanations for the phenomena. You must be willing to understand and accept that as fact. If you go into an investigation with the sole purpose of proving the existence of ghosts, you will do more harm than good to your credibility and to your team. We will deal with how to be an effective skeptical reviewer of your evidence and collection methods later.

CHAPTER SIX
WHAT ARE ORBS? (HINT: NOT A TECHNO BAND)

One of the commonest (and most controversial) anomalies that regularly shows up in many photographs taken at locations believed to be haunted is the *orb*. This typically appears in photographs as a translucent or semitransparent sphere. See figure 1 for an example.

Only a few short years ago, most paranormal investigators believed that orbs represented very strong evidence of paranormal activity. However, as time passed and the

FIGURE 1.

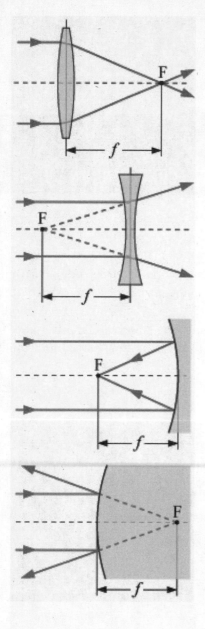

FIGURE 2. POINT F IS THE
FOCAL POINT OF THE LENS.
THE HYPERFOCAL DISTANCE
IS REPRESENTED BY f.

field began to mature, investigators began to better understand the mechanics and inner workings of photography. Today we realize that there are many elements and factors that might cause an orb anomaly to appear in a photograph. These include, but are not limited to, airborne items such as dust and pollen particles, rain, snow, humidity droplets, and even flying insects. Perhaps Raid insect killer might be renamed "Orb Be Gone."

Now, you probably wonder how something so minuscule as a dust speck or pollen grain could create an anomaly in a photo that appears to be hundreds or thousands of times larger. No—the orbs aren't hitting the gym to get "buff." To understand how it really happens, we need to understand how light is focused by a lens.

Okay . . . cue boring, geeky interlude music here. . . . We promise to keep the science lesson brief.

Every camera lens has a rating associated with it known as its *hyperfocal distance (f)*. This property is defined as the distance from the lens element to the point of focus or *focal point* (F). See figure 2 for an illustration. When the camera is focused at point F, any subject within the hyperfocal distance f will appear blurry and out of focus.

Wake up, class!

You can demonstrate this by holding a finger in front of your eye and focusing on it. Next, slowly move your finger toward your eye (not so close that you poke yourself). As your finger gets closer to your eye, you will notice a point at which you can no longer maintain focus. This is the hyperfocal distance of your eye's lens.

As your fingertip goes out of focus, you might notice that it appears to increase in size. This distortion is what causes airborne particles to appear larger than life in photos. Since dust is all around us all of the time, technically speaking there are always going to be dust particles within a lens's hyperfocal distance.

So what causes airborne particles to appear as orbs in certain photos? Quite simply, the intense light from a camera's flash illuminates everything near it—including all the particles floating in the air. If a dust particle happens to be at the right distance from the lens when the flash fires, it can be illuminated and appear as a large, semitransparent sphere.

It's easy enough to demonstrate this concept with a simple experiment in which you create your own false orbs. Now, pay attention—there will be a pop quiz on Friday.

• Get a few sheets of bathroom tissue (unused, please!).

• Turn your digital camera on and charge the flash.

• Wad up the bathroom tissue and gently roll it between your hands or pat it to create a dust cloud.

• Quickly take your camera and snap a flash photo of the resulting dust cloud.

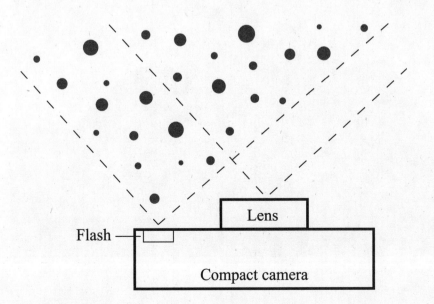

If it's not windy and you time it correctly, when the camera has processed the photo, you should see a large number of "orbs" in the resulting image. (We sure hope it's just dust in the air and that we aren't really all doomed to haunt rolls of Charmin for eternity.)

Seriously, you can now see how dust and other airborne particulates are responsible for the overwhelming majority of orbs that appear in photos.

The dismissal of orbs by most members of the paranormal community is a good example of how the field of research has moved forward and learned from past errors.

One common response we receive when explaining the cause of most photographic orbs is "But it was not dusty in the area when the picture was taken." In reality, dust is everywhere—indoors and out. It doesn't matter how much you clean; it's still

FIGURE 3. NIKON D40X DIGITAL CAMERA
WITH EXTERNAL FLASH ACCESSORY.

there. In fact, using a feather duster is just going to kick up more dust in the air. If you've ever seen a sunbeam shining through a window, you probably noticed countless dust particles moving about in the air currents. Even in sterilized "clean room" environments with filtered air, a small amount of dust is always there. Filters can remove most of the dust but cannot eliminate it totally.

One tip to help reduce false orbs from your photos is to use an external flash unit (if your camera can accept such an accessory, that is). The problem with the built-in flash on most cameras is that it is in very close proximity to the camera lens itself. Because of this, the hyperfocal area is directly illuminated when the flash fires. An external flash can help to resolve this by not directly illuminating airborne particles near the lens.

Of course, good photography starts with being mindful of the conditions under which photos are taken in the first place. Obviously, you are going to get plenty of orbs in your photos if you are taking flash photos in the rain or a snowstorm. Even after a rain shower, many times there will be mist in the air. And indoors, obviously if there is an unusual amount of dust, that too creates an environment unsuitable for collecting photographic evidence. You should refrain from taking photos under these conditions.

While there is good reason to be skeptical of orbs as evidence of paranormal activity, this does not mean that they should be dismissed entirely! There is evidence to suggest that a small percentage of orbs in photos may *possibly* be paranormal in origin.

For example, some orbs in photographs are shown to be partially obscured by distant objects such as trees, walls, large rocks, people, etc. This seems to demonstrate a sense of depth—that the anomaly is at least as far away from the camera as the subject that is obscuring it. If this is the case, it should rule out airborne particles as the source, as it demonstrates that the anomaly cannot be within the hyperfocal distance of the lens. These partially obscured orb photos are not common but are especially noteworthy when you get them.

Also, orbs have been observed by some people with the naked eye. Subjective accounts such as this of course should be carefully critiqued, but sometimes these encounters are corroborated by another eyewitness, or even another investigator's video camera. Evidence from more than one source like this lends credence to the possibility that some orbs really might be something other than particles, dust, rain, or flying insects.

What is an EVP, and can it cause embarrassing stains?

EVP is an acronym standing for electronic voice phenomena (singular: phenomenon). These are the recordings of disembodied voices that are not heard out loud during the time of recording but are heard upon playback of the tape or audio file. They are not to be confused with audible voice phenomena, or AVP, which are a rarer form of communication in which disembodied voices are heard out loud by people present. Recording devices are not needed to hear AVP.

EVP are considered by many to be the most compelling evidence of hauntings, because they're the only kind in which you get some kind of solid, concrete interaction immediately. These phenomena have been reported since the 1940s, and entire factions of paranormal research have been dedicated solely to the collection and understanding of these mysterious recordings.

EVP remain popular among many paranormal investigators for the simple reason that they are relatively easy to capture. All that is required is an inexpensive audio recorder of some type. In recent years, digital voice recorders have come into favor with most EVP researchers. However, older cassette tape recorders and even video camcorders that record on tape may be used as well. EVP happen to be one of the most consistent forms of phenomena we are able to capture.

EVP also comprise one of the most hotly debated forms of evidence while remaining one of the most popular forms as well. In this section, we'll cover the best ways for collecting EVP and tips to eliminate team-member contamination

Before you sit down to gather EVP, it's a good idea to start with a baseline recording of each team member at the location. That is, have each member of your team speak his or her name and a phrase like "Get out" in both regular and whispered tones. If you do this, then when you play back the recording session, you can compare voices captured to the voices of known teammates on-site. This helps to weed out non-EVP voices or false-positive data.

General advice for EVP work

Here is some general advice and guidance to follow when you're doing EVP work:

AVOID WHISPERING ON AN INVESTIGATION.

Whispered voices carry a long distance and are usually higher in frequency that your regular speaking voice. Therefore, a whisper can be picked up by very sensitive recording equipment. On some recorders, you can plug in ear buds or headphones and hear the recording in real time. This also allows you to hear just how sensitive the microphones really are. So the bottom-line rule here is, try to remember not to whisper, and if someone accidentally does, hey—be sure to make note of it on the recording.

ALWAYS IDENTIFY OR "SLATE" YOUR RECORDINGS.

When you press record, always announce the time, location, date, and who is in attendance so that when you review evidence later, you have a working timeline of when exactly an event occurred and who was witness to it. In fact, if you have access to one, a watch or timepiece that shows actual seconds elapsed is even better, as you'll be able to pinpoint the exact time of the event. If other investigators on your team have timepieces with second capabilities, synchronize all of them before you begin your investigation.

During the recording, announce *any* noise that you or a team member may make or hear during that session, for example, "Dave coughed," "Marley whispered," "Patrick farted." Even make note of things that seem mundane or unimportant, such as a dog barking in the distance or a car passing by on the street. All of this becomes important for evidence review. We'd like to think we'll remember everything that happened during the course of an investigation, but more often than not we will not review the evidence for days or sometimes weeks after an event. By tagging the incidents as they happen, we won't forget that just as we asked for a spirit to make its presence known, Patrick farted, and we won't think we've received some form of ethereal flatulence or communication instead.

Remember, not all EVP are recorded as voices. For example, on one investigation the sound of a train whistle could clearly be heard on playback of the recording session, yet there were no train tracks in service anywhere in the area. Phantom footsteps might be recorded when no one present is walking. While it may seem silly, be sure to make notation if anyone's stomach growls. You would not believe how creepy and eerie a person's indigestion sounds when amplified in a recording. You might want to note when someone's stomach growls as an EGP—electronic *gastric* phenomenon!

As avid EVP collectors, we bust people all the time, most notably for whispering during an EVP session. Many natural sounds can appear to be something entirely different upon review. Pattern recognition is when the brain looks for identifiable patterns in visual and auditory stimuli. That's how we can see bunnies and duckies in the clouds or the face of Jesus on a piece of toast or a Dorito. The same principle works with sounds. When reviewing audio recordings, we can impose words or phrases over a common noise and convince ourselves we are hearing responses to our questions.

Here are some common noises that can be misconstrued during evidence review: coughing, sneezing, sniffing, scratching your finger across the recorder's microphone, the sound of a camera whirring or flashing, etc. If you take a picture during a recording session, call it out and say, "Flash!" so that any mechanical sounds your equipment makes are not mistaken for a weak, quiet voice. A mechanical whir can sound like a "Yes" or "Help" when played back.

DO NOT TAUNT OR PROVOKE.

Be respectful at all times. Ghosts should be treated as though they were still living people. How would you like somebody to come into your home and try to communicate with you or your family? Would you want somebody barging in and bullying them or being rude? Would you want to be screamed at or have someone demand that you perform tricks to amuse people? Unless you're an exhibit in a sideshow, the answer is probably no. Spirits don't *have* to respond. They are not there for our amusement or to act upon command. Make your requests and questions simple, kind, and polite. If you are rude or discourteous, you will most likely send the ghost packing, and it will find someone else to communicate with in a different room. If you're polite and considerate, you're likely to get a much better EVP response while you're investigating.

Let's just cite a hypothetical example. A team investigated a beautiful antebellum-style mansion from the 1800s in Georgia. When doing EVP, the team began demanding things of the spirits using modern-day terms and language with a tremendous lack of manners.

"What's your name?" they asked gruffly. "What did you die from?" they barked out. "Are you stuck here?"

At this point, you can almost imagine the resident ghosts standing there in utter horror at these rude people who had intruded upon their home and now made demands of them.

Try to put yourself in the mind-set of the spirits and the age they come from. Rather than being obnoxious about it, attempt to understand what you're dealing with, and you might get better responses. When people taunt, bad things have been known to happen. People have reported being hit with flying objects. In more extreme cases, people have been physically pushed down flights of stairs. Mary Ann Winkowski, the real-life Ghost Whisperer, says, "As in life, so in death." If the spirit was a jerk in life, he's going to be a jerk on the other side. If you push him, he's going to push back . . . so be careful.

ASK SIMPLE QUESTIONS.

If you're dealing with ghosts from the 1800s and you begin an EVP session by saying, "I have this piece of recording technology in my hand that will record your voice in a frequency that allows me to hear what you have to say upon playback," then it is possible you might confuse the spirit. Someone who lived in the 1800s isn't going to be familiar with today's technology and terms. Envision the resident spirits looking at one another and saying, "What is he talking about?" Use the KISS method—keep it simple, stupid!

Try this instead, "The machine in my hand may be able to hear your voice. If you see the light, please come up, yell, scream, let me know that you're there. I'll try to help you." If you're dealing with a spirit of someone who lived before the Industrial Revolution, it may not be as familiar with "machine." Some investigators instead choose to use the term "contraption," which was a more prevalent term used prior to the twentieth century. The simpler you keep it, the better the chances you have of communicating effectively with the spirits in these locations.

USING VOICE-ACTIVATED RECORDERS VERSUS JUST RUNNING THE RECORDER THE WHOLE TIME.

Voice-activated recording, or VOX, is one method of recording EVP. Voice-activated recorders automatically turn on when they pick up a sound. The issue with many of these recorders is that they have a tendency to start recording a split second after someone begins speaking. This means you don't always pick up the entire word or phrase as it is being spoken. Since most EVP are one to three words long, you might miss all or part of what could have been a very compelling piece of evidence. Some of the most impressive EVP are captured right at the start of the session.

Another problem is that voice activation is triggered only when the microphone detects a sound above a certain level. Many EVP are faint and fall below the necessary threshold to trigger recording. As such, you may not capture every voice or sound— paranormal or otherwise—that occurs during the recording session.

VOX recording seems like a good idea on the surface. It would stand to reason that it might drastically reduce the amount of audio to review. However, if you're using VOX recording, you might miss some of the fainter EVP, and this issue outweighs its usefulness in our opinion. It is recommended by most EVP specialists to simply turn on your recorder, let it run, and capture everything.

TRY TWO METHODS OF EVP COLLECTING.

First, ask somebody to run the recorder the whole time and then let him review his own evidence. Sure, he'll sit a room for four hours with headphones on, hearing the static of white noise and waiting for a ghost voice to come out and say "Hey," but then again, a lot of ghost-hunting tasks are tedious. Then, another person can do what's referred to as short-burst EVP sessions, as recommended by EVP experts Mark and Debby Constantino. Turn on the recorder and record a session of no more than five to ten minutes that you will immediately review. It's an important and very crucial method of EVP collection, because the questions tend to be "Can I help you?" "Would you like to cross over?" "Do you have a message you'd like to pass on to somebody here?" Since you listen back immediately and can hear possible responses, it's a lot easier to try to conduct a two-way conversation.

Our team went into one room and did three EVP sweeps. The first two EVP sweeps got absolutely nothing. On the third EVP sweep, we were convinced we weren't going to get anything and decided to move out of the room. Just as we said, "We're getting ready to leave," a voice clearly whispered, "Don't leave." Of course, we were boneheads and left, because we didn't stop to listen to what we'd recorded. It was just a three-minute EVP recording, but if we'd listened to it on the spot, we might have had more interaction. Instead, no one listened to the recording for a week. Think of what we missed! We could have had what we are all looking for in this paranormal field. It could have been a true connection.

The Constantinos will synchronize two voice-activated recorders. They will start them at the same time and ask five to ten questions. Then they'll look to see if there is a discrepancy in the recording time. If Mark's recording is two minutes and Debby's is two minutes and thirty seconds, they will begin by reviewing her recorder in hopes that it picked up on something that Mark's may not have.

DO NOT TALK OVER ONE ANOTHER DURING A SCHEDULED EVP SESSION.
When someone on your team is doing an EVP session, don't interrupt or talk over him or her. Also, allow time for a response. Don't be that person on the team who talks nonstop during an investigation. It's hard to do an effective EVP session while others continue to talk and walk around the room and create all types of disturbances. There have been instances of a spirit responding to a line of questioning but someone else in the room being so loud that you could not make out what the spirit said. Such recordings have to be disregarded altogether.

Pace your questioning and give the spirit time to respond. Since it has to use energy from you, the air, and your devices, often you won't get an immediate response, so conduct your EVP session something like this:

> "Hi, this is Dave. I'm in the Christmas Room
> at Rolling Hills Sanitarium." *(Pause.)*
>
> "Can you please tell me your name?" *(Pause.)*
>
> "What year is it?" *(Pause.)*
>
> "Why are you here?" *(Pause.)*
>
> "How can we help you?" *(Pause.)*

SHOULD YOU USE AN EXTERNAL MICROPHONE OR THE INTERNAL MICROPHONE THAT IS BUILT INTO THE UNIT?

This is a question that can cause quite a heated debate. There are a few pros and cons on each side of the debate. Try using both methods and find which one yields the best results for you. Some people will say you need the external microphone because it will give a cleaner recording and there is less chance of recording the internal workings of the recorder, causing false positives or audio pattern recognition. Purists argue that you can get much better results with the white noise the internal microphone picks up on. They claim that the spirits don't have vocal cords or voice boxes, so they need a base sound to manipulate to create a connection. We authors have heard EVP from both sources . . . as well as garbage from both. It's pretty much a personal choice and should be tested by you and your investigative team for the most effective results.

DO YOU NEED AN EXPENSIVE AUDIO RECORDER?

No. EVP specialists Mark and Debby Constantino get amazing results and do not use the super-high-tech expensive recorders. They suggest basic models that can cost between $39 and $100 each. The more expensive, fancier units have noise compensators in them, and sometimes they end up filtering themselves out, removing any EVP you may capture.

In closing, just remember that when you're doing EVP work you should be patient, polite, respectful, and knowledgeable about the location and the spirits you hope to communicate with. In the end you can yield much better results than most investigators by employing these simple techniques.

CHAPTER EIGHT
THE USE OF PSYCHICS AND MEDIUMS

Did you ever know something was going to happen before it happened? Were you ever thinking about a friend you had not heard from in some time, only to have him call you moments later, and you knew it was him before you even saw the caller ID? If so, you may have a psychic ability. They say—the "they" who know everything—that we all have it in us.

Most psychics believe we're all born with these inherent "sixth sense" abilities. But just as some people are naturally gifted at sports or math or music, so are certain individuals gifted with a superior knack beyond the five normal senses of sight, sound, touch, smell, and taste.

Some paranormal investigators shun the use of psychics. They believe that because psychic impressions are subjective and anecdotal (yeah, yeah . . . fifty-cent words) and thus can't really be physically proven, they aren't useful during paranormal investigations. However, psychics can be of use when their senses and feelings can be backed up by evidence on the instruments you chose to use. For example, the psychic can instruct the paranormal investigators on where to set up their equipment and take measurements. If strange activity is measured in that particular location, it validates what the psychic is feeling. This approach is really a win-win situation for both sides and is pretty cool when it happens.

Those folks who are nonbelievers in psychic abilities will often mutter that if psychic abilities are real, why aren't psychics using their skills for financial gain by gambling or investing in the stock market? Comedian Jay Leno is famously quoted as saying, "I keep waiting to see the headline 'Psychic Wins Lottery.'" Most psychics have heard this question all their lives and merely roll their eyes.

Let's just be clear that no psychic is 100 percent accurate 100 percent of the time. In fact, certain studies suggest that even the best psychics are accurate only 30 percent of the time. While it may seem unimpressive that they are wrong more often than they are right, the mere fact that they are right any percentage of time is of note. After all, we humans aren't perfect in any endeavor we undertake. Using athletes again for comparison, even the best all-star sports figures have days when their performance is mediocre or even below par. Since science doesn't recognize psychic abilities as valid, people automatically expect psychics to be 100 percent accurate. When they aren't, people think claims of psychic talents are delusional or outright fraudulent.

The three of us have each witnessed numerous demonstrations of psychic abilities that, in our opinion, are quite valid. While it's important always to maintain a healthy dose of skepticism, the purpose of this book is not to debate one side or the other. For the sake of argument, we'll assume the position that psychic abilities may be real aspects of human consciousness based on our own experiences.

DIFFERENT TYPES OF PSYCHIC ABILITIES

There are many different types of psychic abilities that fall into various categories. For example, the psychic ability known as *precognition* allows a psychic (or as many prefer to be called "sensitive") to know the future, whereas the ability known as *clairvoyance,* sometimes also called *remote viewing,* allows the subject to mentally visualize events and locations from a distance. A similar ability known as *clairaudience* allows the person to hear remote events. Some psychics even claim to be able to converse directly with the spirit world. These subjects are typically referred to as *mediums.*

These various abilities may be applied to paranormal investigation of hauntings in a lot of ways. Many believe that the clairvoyant and clairaudient may be able to see and hear events that happened many years ago, like watching a video recording. A retroactive form of precognition known as *postcognition* or *retrocognition* allows the sensitive to peer back in time: to see history. People who have these sensitivities can be of a lot of help during an investigation. In the case of a haunting that is occurring where few to no historical records exist, the sensitive can often provide the essential (or missing) information that connects the dots and explains why that location may be experiencing paranormal activity.

Mediums, with their ability to talk directly to ghosts and spirits, are of obvious benefit to your paranormal research team. Famed ghost hunter Professor Hans Holzer, Ph.D., believes that the only two items required to conduct a ghost hunt are an audio recording device and a trance medium.

WHAT IS A TRANCE MEDIUM?

A medium who works under trance will channel or allow a spirit to communicate directly through his or her body while under hypnosis. In essence, the trance medium allows him- or herself to become temporarily "possessed" by outside forces. When this connection is made, the trance medium's voice may change and he or she may take on the characteristics and/or mannerisms of the person whose spirit he or she is channeling. During the trance session, your team can ask direct questions of the spiritual entity, making notes on and of course taking audio recordings of the entire experience. When the medium awakens, he or she doesn't always have a memory of the session or what was said. At the conclusion of the trance session, the details revealed are checked out to determine if they are accurate. Did such a person once exist? Are there historical documents to back up what the trance medium said? All this must be confirmed through further investigation by you and your team. Trance mediums are not very common, as many psychics are a bit skeeved out by the idea of allowing their body to be controlled by outside forces. And seriously . . . can you blame them?

So how do you know if someone is truly psychic? Good question! The solution is quite simple—put him or her to the test! Take the person into a location completely "cold," that is, without her knowing anything about the location or the events that happened there. See what she can come up with on her own. In the case of a well-known historical location, obviously there is the possibility that this subject may already know details of the events that took place there. So it's best to test someone's psychic abilities in a location that is not publicized.

Remember again that a lot of psychics will be wrong more often than they are exact. It's really important to allow some flexibility in terms of their accuracy.

Just as it's true with anyone you meet, not all people claiming to have psychic abilities are honest. Yeah, we said it. Unfortunately, outright fraud exists within the paranormal community. When taking a psychic into a haunted location, it's quite possible he may have done his "homework" ahead of time to gain premature knowledge about a location and history of a haunting. Then when brought there, he might reveal the intricate details of his research, claiming he is receiving them from the spirit world. This is simply cheating, and it gives everyone in the paranormal community—psychics and investigators alike—a really bad name.

Many investigators go to great lengths to deliberately cloud details of an investigation beforehand to make sure the psychic/sensitive doesn't have any knowledge ahead of time that might "taint" the investigation. Some believe that the only true way to test a psychic is to conduct what is known in science as a double-blind experiment. That is, not only will the psychic not have prior knowledge of a location, but you as the investigator will not have any prior knowledge either.

Another form of psychic ability known as *telepathy* is the act of reading a person's mind. It's believed that some psychics may either deliberately or inadvertently utilize telepathy to read the minds of the investigators, property owners, and other people present during the investigation who might have information about the location. While it's even amazing to think that someone has the ability to read minds—that would be a paranormal event in and of itself—it's not the objective or goal of investigating a haunting, and a double-blind experiment is the means to eliminate this as a possibility.

If you choose to use psychics within your investigations and include them as a part of your team, it's important to remain skeptical, but not so much as to become cynical—that is, a complete disbeliever. Give the psychic a chance to prove to you that he or she is genuinely gifted. You may find a true psychic who will prove to be an invaluable asset on your investigations and help you connect with the spirit world on a deeper level.

CHAPTER NINE
SAFE HEX: PROTECTION FOR YOU AND YOUR TEAM

Many people overlook the role of protection in the investigative process or deem it unnecessary. We all hear stories of spirits that follow people home from an investigation, but we always assume it's something that will never happen to us. This couldn't be further from the truth. No one really knows what may or may not be encountered at a ghost hunt, so it is always best to be prepared for any eventuality. Because of this, we need to discuss the many uses and types of protection.

We have taken a look at some of the most effective ways to protect you and your team, and here are some suggestions we've compiled.

Commonly used prayers

Let's start by discussing the different blessings and prayers that many teams have found effective. Included in this list are Christian, Wiccan, and nontraditional methods that can allow for each member of your team to interject his or her own belief system into the blessings of protection.

Of the most powerful Christian prayers, we suggest the following:

THE LORD'S PRAYER
Our Father, who art in heaven,
Hallowed be thy Name.
Thy kingdom come.
Thy will be done,
On earth as it is in heaven.
Give us this day our daily bread.
And forgive us our trespasses,
As we forgive those who trespass against us.
And lead us not into temptation,

But deliver us from evil.
For thine is the kingdom, and the power,
and the glory, forever and ever.
Amen.

THE PRAYER TO SAINT MICHAEL
Saint Michael the Archangel, defend us in battle;
Be our protection against the wickedness and snares of the devil.
May God rebuke him, we humbly pray:
And do thou, O Prince of the heavenly host, by the power of God,
Thrust into hell Satan and all the evil spirits
Who prowl about the world seeking the ruin of souls.
Amen.

Psychic/medium and ghost hunter Chip Coffey offers up this simple yet effective prayer to close each investigation:

In the Name of the Lord, Jesus Christ,
no entities are allowed to follow me from this location.
By the Power of God, I command you to remain here.

Here is a final religiously based prayer we will offer that addresses your angel guides and guardian angels and can also be very effective:

Angel of God, guardian dear
To whom God's love commits me here
Ever this day be at my side,
To light, to guard, to rule and guide.
Amen.

A good number of members of the paranormal societies are from a pagan or Wicca background. For you we offer the following:

WICCA PROTECTION CHANT
God and Goddess of the skies,
Please respond to my cries.
Lift me up in your strong arms,
Away from those who seek me harm.
Shield me from the awful rage

That shall face me day to day.
Help me be strong in what I do,
And help my heart remain true.
Give me strength to face each day,
And the hardships before me lain.
Let those whom I love, love me in return,
And every day let me learn.
I bid you both my spirits keep,
While I'm awake and asleep.
So mote it be!

The following is offered up from Regan Vacknitz of the paranormal group APART, in Washington state. It is a protective measure that you can do as a team that leaves an opening for each member to adapt it to his or her own religious beliefs.

> We are here to communicate with the spirits that are present. We are not here to harm you or change your environment in any way. We wish only to give you a voice you haven't had in a long time. We respect your ground, but you need to respect our mind, body, and soul.

Then take a moment of silence, allowing those from various faiths to pray, meditate, or protect themselves however they wish.

At the end of the investigation they do the following closing:

> We thank the spirits for coming forward and sharing their experiences with us. This is where you belong. Do not follow us home. This is your roots, your ground; you need to remain here.

Regan offers this final piece of advice:

> The best way to protect yourself is by maintaining a healthy, happy, positive outlook. If any, and I mean any of the team members are having a bad day, send them home. Their negativity leaves you open as a target. Even if they are not negative by nature, a bad day is just that . . . a bad day. If at anytime anything feels "off," end the investigation. There's no reason to push forward if it feels wrong. You will only attract negativity.

The next nontraditional prayer is from Diana Cannon, a paranormal investigator:

RING OF PROTECTION PRAYER
In the Name of All That is Goodness and Light,
Surround Our Circle in the White Light of Holy
Protection.
We Ask That No Harm Befalls or Follows the Pro-
tected Circle
And That Our Quest Benefit All Who Are Among Us.
In the Name of All That Is Goodness and Light,
We Thank Thee for Your Protection of Holy White
Light.
Amen.

In Diana's online blog, she also offers the following suggestions for further protection:

CRUCIFIX

Be careful of what you say in the form of a question when trying to make contact. Show respect with please and thank you and never place any demands on the unseen or unexplained. You may ask for a response like please make a noise or move that table for us again. But if you try to provoke, and make statements like, "I dare you to do something! Touch me. Touch any of us . . . we are not afraid of you," is when you open a door that you have no idea what you just invited into your life.

Diana raises a very good point about trying to communicate with the spirits. Never invite spirits to communicate through you or to enter you. Be careful with the way you phrase your questions or requests and do not open yourselves for an attachment. You also give them permission to do so by engaging in automatic writing, channeling, and the use of a Ouija board.

We are very careful when trying to open a dialogue with the other side and suggest using the following statements as a means of engagement:

Please feel free to speak out loud or communicate to us through our machines, either by showing yourself or making yourself be heard. I do not give permission for you to enter my mind or my body under any circumstances. The machines we use may be able to see you or hear your voice. Please speak as loudly as you can, and we will try to talk to you.

Leave channeling and the use of automatic writing or divination to those who have spent a good portion of their lives learning and understanding how to control their psychic abilities. If you are just in the beginning stages of your psychic development, it is never advisable to allow spirits to have control of you in any capacity.

Use of charms and religious medallions

Most of the people we deal with in the field rely heavily on four main religious charms or medallions for protection:

THE CRUCIFIX
A blessed crucifix is believed to hold a very powerful protective field of influence over the person who wields it, whether it is an actual crucifix that you carry or a pendant that you wear as a necklace.

THE SAINT MICHAEL MEDALLION
Saint Michael is considered one of the most powerful of the angels and is revered for his ability to protect us from Satan and his army. He is also considered the patron saint of policemen.

THE SAINT MICHAEL MEDALLION

ST. BENEDICTINE MEDAL

ROSARY

THE SAINT BENEDICTINE MEDAL

The following is a partial list of the purposes of the medal of Saint Benedict:

1. It wards off from both the soul and the body all dangers arising from the devil.
2. It obtains protection and aid for persons tormented by the evil spirit and in temptation against holy purity.
3. It procures assistance in the hour of death.

This medal has long been regarded as very effective in protecting its wearers against demonic attacks and securing a number of special graces. The medal itself is believed to provide a constant silent prayer of protection to the owner. The power of the medallion comes from the inscriptions and images upon it.

Around the image of Saint Benedict are these words in Latin, "May his presence protect us in the hour of death." The reverse of the medal shows the image of the cross. Around the margin are the initials of Latin words forming verses that are supposed to have originated with the holy father Benedict himself. The English translation is "Get behind me, Satan; Never suggest vain thoughts to me. The cup you offer is evil; Drink the poison yourself!" In the angles formed by the arms of the cross are the letters *C, S, P,* and *B,* signifying "Cross of the holy Father Benedict." The letters on the cross have this meaning: "May the holy Cross be my light; And may the Dragon never be my guide."

There is no set way of carrying or applying the medal. It may be worn around the neck, attached to the rosary, or carried in your purse or pocket.

THE ROSARY

The rosary is also a very revered tool for the religious to take with them on an investigation.

It is always suggested that the above-mentioned items be blessed, which can be done by taking them to your local church and asking the priest, pastor, or leader to bless them.

Remember that for these items to be most effectual, you must have a belief in them and the religious background that they come from. Otherwise you may as well carry a Superman doll and some licorice. Without belief there is no real power.

OTHER USEFUL/HELPFUL TOOLS

For those of you who are not of a religious nature or lean more toward the Wiccan/pagan or New Age movement, there are quite a few effective tools for you to apply to ghost hunting and protection.

The following is a brief list of crystals that can be carried or used on an investigation:

Amethyst
Carnelian
Citrine
Fluorite
Garnet
Jade
Jasper
Jet
Kunzite
Labradorite
Obsidian
Onyx
Peridot
Prehnite
Quartz
Rose quartz
Smoky quartz
Tourmaline

Crystals each have their own properties and can be used in different ways. Check with a local metaphysical shop or gemologist for a rundown of each stone's power and use. Some crystals are also very useful in trying to communicate with the other side, and when placed on paranormal equipment, they have been known to increase its effectiveness.

Smudging is also a very popular method of protection before and after an investigation. Smudging is a ritual of purification by smoke and was used extensively by Native Americans. Smudging can also be traced back to most ancient cultures. They burned things of various types for many spiritual reasons. Each scent was thought to have a different purpose. For example, the scents of burning incense, frankincense, and myrrh were thought to "please the gods." Native Americans use various herbs that are thought to purify a person, place, or thing by application and interaction of the smoke with the item. A space in

SMUDGE STICKS

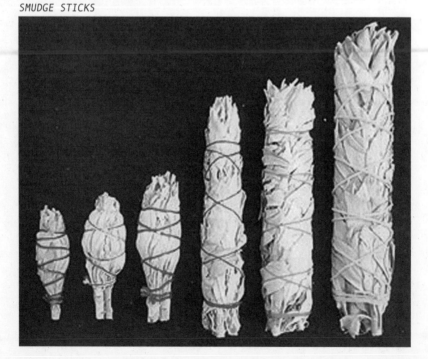

which a ritual is to take place is smudged with smoke, as are all the ritual instruments and the people who pass into the space.

Smudge sticks are hand-held bundles of herbs that are set on fire. After a few moments of burning, they are blown out so that they smolder and create smoke. The smudge stick is then carried around the area you wish to cleanse or waved around the person or persons you wish to purify. Sometimes the smoke is directed to the corners of the room or toward an individual using a feather and fanning the smoke. This ensures that the person or space is thoroughly covered by the smoke.

Herbs commonly used in smudging are sages, cedar, or sweet grass, and they can be obtained at most metaphysical shops and some health food stores. Sage is believed to drive negative spirits away, sweet grass is said to attract good spirits and energies (so typically sage is burned before sweet grass), and cedar is used when expelling negativity and attracting positive forces.

In our interviews with teams, individuals, and other experts in the paranormal field, it was universally agreed upon that at no time should an investigator experiment with drugs or alcohol on an investigation. It is strongly believed that this can leave you open to many forms of unpleasant interactions with the spirit or demonic realm and should be avoided at all costs.

You should also remove yourself immediately from an investigation if you are feeling any fear or negative feelings. These emotions seem to feed the negative forces and can possibly lead to unwanted attachments and interference from the spiritual realm.

Investigating the paranormal is an exciting activity, but you should make a conscious choice to follow a protection ritual before and after any investigation. It should be something you approach professionally and with commitment, not take lightly or with a glib attitude. There is a real danger in exposing yourself to the paranormal, and that should always be considered. As with any hobby, there are certain risks involved, and certain levels of precaution should be taken. You wouldn't go skateboarding without protective gear or jump out of a plane without a parachute, so don't skimp on procedure here either.

We have all been asked at one time or another whether you can be too protected on a paranormal investigation by wearing medallions, smudging, protecting yourself in prayer . . . that it may actually prevent you from experiencing any paranormal activity. There is some validity to that thought. However, as with most things in the paranormal, intent seems to dictate results. The prayers, smudging, and medallions are more to keep you protected from negative influences. Ninety-nine percent of the spirits you'll encounter don't appear to be malevolent in nature and are often misunderstood. People mistake books being thrown or hair getting pulled as negative when, in fact, it might be the only way a spirit can make its presence known. Using the abovementioned forms of protection should do nothing more than remove negative activity. If you're clearly defining your goal of investigating, then your intent should make it clear to those willing entities that they will be able to communicate with you.

INTERVIEW WITH A PSYCHIC/MEDIUM

Since many investigators believe themselves to be sensitives or have psychic abilities, we wanted to seek advice about psychic protection on investigations from a famous psychic ghost hunter. We asked Minnesota-based Echo Bodine a few questions about the subject.

Q: Echo, what precautions do you take before or during investigations to assure your safety and psychic protection from attachments?

A: Psychic attachments are way overrated. They're not as common as everyone is making them out to be these days. Asking the universe to clear our minds, our bodies, and our souls helps immensely.

Q: Do you meditate?

A: Yes, throughout the day and before I go to bed.

Q: Do you cover yourself in white light?

A: I visualize the white light coming from the center of myself and I will consciously take several breaths, and each time I do that, I see the white light getting bigger and eventually surrounding me.

Q: Do you wear a tinfoil hat [to protect against mind control or mind reading]?

A: Only to church on Easter.

Q: Do you drink goats' blood?

A: No, I'm gluten intolerant.

Q: Are there *any* concerns people should have about safety on ghost-hunting investigations?

A: Seriously, I do have real concerns for people involving themselves in this field of study. My biggest concern for anyone doing this kind of work is that it can be exhausting on the body. Most ghost hunters go in with their body completely open psychically so that they can sense, feel, or see the apparitions. Most of us are so used to doing that that we don't take into account how draining it can be on our body's energy.

The other factor to take into account is that earthbound spirits often take energy from the people in the room in order to materialize or make their energy stronger so that they can show up on the equipment. Every time my brother and I finished a ghost clearing, we were starving and always headed for the nearest fast-food drive-through.

So here are some tips to help keep your energy intact and make sure you're not taking anyone home with you:

Get some kind of outfit together that becomes your "ghost-hunting suit" and wear that every time you go out on a job. It's not the clothing that protects you but the attitude you *become* when you put it on. We used to kid each other about getting some kind of astronaut suit that would protect us from getting slimed psychically. It's a mindset. It mentally prepares you to step into your power as the authority in the room.

When the job is finished, open a window and burn some sage or palo santo [holy wood from Peru] or spray some Florida water. Be sure to spray or smoke yourself when you are done, asking the universe to clear every part of your body, mind, and soul.

My experience has been that most ghosts do not follow you home. They don't like to change, which is one of the reasons why they are stuck. But to be on the cautious side, ask the universe to clear all the space at least three feet around you and cut any energy cords that the entity might have attached to you.

Get out of the clothes as soon as you can and hang them outside to clear out.

The most important tip to remember is that you are the one with the body, you are the one with the power, and you are the one in charge of this experience.

If you are feeling spacy afterward, you need to get grounded, so do anything that reminds you that you are living in a psychical body, i.e., eat, sing, dance, go to a movie, go outside and spend time in nature. Take a shower or bath. Visualize roots coming out of your feet and going down into the earth. Carry rocks in your pockets. The main thing is to get as many of your physical senses going as possible: taste, touch, smell, see, feel.

And last, allow extra time to get a good night's sleep. Take a couple of magnesium tablets (nature's tranquilizer) before going to bed to relax your mind and body.

CHAPTER TEN
DEMONOLOGY: EXCITING AND FUN?

Oh, yeah, baby! Finally a chapter with some bite. Everyone knows that demonologists get all the money, attention, and fame and are the rock stars of the paranormal field. For just $6.66 we can show you how you too can be a butt-kicking demon warrior and win friends and influence people!

Demonology has become one of the most popular aspects of paranormal investigating and in our opinion one that should not be taken lightly. Demonology is not something to be viewed as "extreme ghost hunting" or "cool." It is the most dangerous aspect of investigating and should be considered as such.

Real demonologists study the field for years; they know every aspect of it and are well versed in the knowledge of demons and how they work and affect people, as well as their role in theology and the studies of most major religions. Reading a few books or watching *The Exorcist* a hundred times doesn't qualify you as a demonologist any more than watching police dramas on TV makes me an officer of the law.

We wish to acknowledge this part of the field but want to make it clear that this area of development is not for just anyone. According to the experts, you must have received a real calling to participate in this aspect of the paranormal. It is not glamorous, it is not going to make you rich or popular, and it can endanger you and the people you love and care about. Demonologists who are gifted and called into service to do this work are often single and won't even own pets, as dark forces can affect animals as well as loved ones. To enter this particular field, you must understand that it is a major undertaking and involves more than just you. It can have adverse reactions on relationships and other involvements.

Many people are weekend warriors and aren't excited by the prospect of an actual investigation; they want an amped-up experience in which they face dark forces and malevolent spirits. They feel that this is exciting and will hold their attention longer. This couldn't be further from the truth. Ghost hunting is quieter than you think. Very few hauntings actually deal with demonic forces, and most times when spirits appear to be dark or evil, it's simply a misunderstanding of the activity. Just because you feel a touch, a dish is pushed off a table and breaks, or loud noises are made doesn't mean that you are dealing with forces of evil. A lot of times it is simply the way spirits are able to let their presence be known. It takes a lot of work and energy for entities to be heard or felt, and they may not know how forceful their actions will come through or appear to us. So many people jump the gun and assume they are bad spirits.

Shadow people are also often associated with or judged as evil entities, since they are black and menacing. We have found that most shadow-people sightings are nothing more than tricks of the eyes and low-light surroundings. Again, it may be that these entities have only enough energy to appear in that form and cannot fully manifest. We don't really know how ghosts appear, and if they draw energy from us, energy sources, or surroundings, we can only guess as to the abilities they have. Very few shadow-people encounters are ever menacing or troublesome. Most are fleeting. Shadow people seem as frightened or as curious about us as we are about them.

The study of demons and demonology should be a long and well-researched process. We suggest speaking to well-known demonologists or attending their lectures. Ask them if they believe this is a good field for you to enter into.

Demonologists are the people who are called in when things get bad, and they have made many sacrifices to do what they do and to be a part of this type of investigation. They have also spent years making associations with leaders in many of the religious fields and know other experts to whom they can go for information and guidance.

This chapter isn't meant to frighten you away from the subject. It is meant more as a moment to pause and reflect on your decisions and how they can affect not only your life but also the lives of those around you. We only ask that you not rush into this particular study or expertise. Again, we encourage those of you just starting in the field to reach out and get to know the professionals. Most of them will be happy to assist you. If they can't, they know who can in your area. Don't feel you need to be the Chosen One. Instead, utilize those who came before you and have a vast knowledge. That's what they are there for.

Take baby steps when beginning your journey into becoming a paranormal investigator. You have to walk before you can run, and you have to have a firm grasp and understanding of the basics of investigating before you decide to square off with the minions of darkness. Get a feel for your strengths and see where the field leads you before you make major decisions like facing Satan and his pals. It's not all it's cracked up to be. Oh, sure, your head may spin around, and that's always popular at parties. Levitation is cool, but when you start barfing pea-green soup and speaking in deep, creepy voices, your friends will tire of you and move on to something else.

CHAPTER ELEVEN
A HEALTHY DOSE OF SKEPTICISM

At this point, we should address the difference between a skeptic and a cynic. Many people mistake one for the other or brand themselves incorrectly.

The dictionary defines a *skeptic* in the following ways:

1. a person who questions the validity or authenticity of something purporting to be factual.

2. a person who maintains a doubting attitude, as toward values, plans, statements, or the character of others.

Skeptics are people who question everything until all possibilities are exhausted. They examine the claims, the people, and the environment of every situation. As the authors of this book, we are believers in the paranormal, we are investigators, and we are paranormal detectives who seek the truth and try to separate fact from fiction. We are also skeptics, each one of us. Personal experiences drew us into the field and continue to push us to find the answers for ourselves and those who come to us for help. We know what we know and have experienced many things; however, that doesn't mean that every bad smell is a demon, every bang in the wall is old Uncle Bob letting you know he is still around, and every creaky door is a shadow person coming to steal your soul.

Many people look at the term *skeptical* or *skeptic* as a negative or dirty word in our field of practice, when in fact more people in the field need to be skeptical. It does you, your team, and the entire investigative field harm if you are willing to believe or fall for every claim made. As a responsible investigator, you should adopt and adhere to the following principles: always be questioning, always seek the truth, and always remain objective. If you allow your own personal beliefs to influence an investigation, you can taint the entire process. You can be skeptical and respectful at the same time, and that is very important to your client. Remember, to them this can be a very frightening situation or, at the very least, unpleasant. It takes many people a long time to seek help, and if you are quick to dismiss them, then you may be doing more harm than good.

As skeptics we have to assume that most ghostly claims are simply misconceptions or products of overactive imaginations. Does that mean we think people are trying to mislead or trick us? No, it means that as they lie awake at night, in the dark, and they hear an unfamiliar sound or view a strange anomaly, they are confused. They may be fans of the many TV shows about ghost hunting, and their imaginations get the best of them. They start leaping to conclusions. It is our job as investigators to remain objective and review the situations, stories, and surroundings. More than half of paranormal claims can be dismissed within minutes of arriving at a location. Doors that are known to swing open or closed are often found to be hung incorrectly. Or the house may have settled over the years and the foundation is a bit uneven, so the weight distribution of doors or cabinets can make them swing open. It has nothing to do with spirit activity and more to do with poor workmanship or sudden breezes. Skeptics want to get to the bottom of claims and find answers.

Now we will take a quick look at cynics. No amount of evidence will ever satisfy a real cynic. Jesus Christ could walk into a crowded room and start handing out loaves and fishes, and the cynic would believe that witnesses have been given a mass hypnotic suggestion. Cynics will dismiss and ridicule people whose beliefs differ from their own. Many self-proclaimed skeptics in the field are nothing more than hyped-up cynical bullies who will speak louder and more aggressively than and try to intimidate those who have had experiences or believe in the paranormal. Many have said to us, "I would love real proof of the paranormal and would welcome someone showing me an actual example of the supernatural." However, they will interrupt you, ignore you, or belittle your every effort to share thoughts, ideas, and evidence with them. They believe that if something cannot be reproduced, it must be dismissed.

Skeptics and cynics both question, both show doubt toward the validity of a statement or claim. The difference seems to be that whereas a skeptic seeks the truth and delivers a well-thought-out and objective viewpoint, remaining open to the possibility that the paranormal exists, the cynic seeks only to convert you to his beliefs and will disavow anything that he has predetermined as impossible.

A good investigator will always be open-minded. That doesn't mean you have to buy into all claims, but at least hear what the claims are. Repeat them back to the client to verify that you understand them correctly, and then begin to break down the facts as you know them.

Giving the client an understanding of the facts is often a helpful first step to investigating. If we can educate people about the common false positives that create most reported hauntings, they can, in effect, investigate on their own and eliminate many of the misleading circumstances that are often associated with a haunting. If after an evaluation of the claims we still can't find explanations for the phenomena, it's time to pursue a more in-depth second investigation, involving more of the team and the family.

Being skeptical is one of the most important tools you can bring to any investigation. It shows the client that you are thoughtful, intelligent, and methodical in your process. No one, not even the believers, wants to feel as if you are more in awe of the situation than they are. You must convey a sense of confidence that answers can and will be found. Many of the people you encounter are conflicted. They want something to be going on in their home or workplace so they don't feel crazy, but they also want to know the truth and are hoping they aren't dealing with a trapped loved one or angry spirit. They want to be reassured that answers will be found, that action will be taken, and that they are in good hands.

Over the past few years, we have had more reports of damage by groups that are overzealous and want only to prove the existence of the paranormal. Many groups start with the sole purpose in mind of finding activity and documenting it in hopes that they can sell their story or become the next television paranormal celebrities. They take over a home and create more drama than was ever reported, making families uneasy and exaggerating their findings to try to sensationalize their group. This is a horrible mistake. It can do irreparable damage to your reputation and that of your group and the entire field in general.

If you are in this field for glamour, excitement, fame, and fortune, you are in the wrong place. If you are in the field to prove to yourself the existence of the paranormal or ghosts and have no real intention of helping people, then you need to find another hobby or stick to investigating haunted hotels, cemeteries, and locations that encourage that activity. If you are in this field to educate yourself and enlighten others, then do so in a respectful way and use common sense when approaching people dealing with these issues. The field doesn't need more goofballs going off half-cocked and looking to create a name for themselves.

Skeptics are an important part of a paranormal investigation. They shouldn't be looked down upon, as they challenge you and make you raise the bar of excellence. The teams and individuals who rise to this challenge will excel and become respected leaders in the field. It's that respect that will create longevity for you and your group and will keep the requests for investigations flowing. Word of mouth is our best friend or worst enemy in investigating—it can open doors to you that others may never see. On the other hand, it can kill a team and any chance it may have ever had of being allowed to document amazing cases. Remain even-tempered and logical, and always represent yourself and your team with patience, kindness, and a healthy dose of skepticism, and you will find an inviting field of research that can be very rewarding.

CHAPTER TWELVE
REVIEWING YOUR EVIDENCE

Do we stand a ghost of a chance of catching paranormal activity? Let's take a look at the most important aspect of the investigation and at times the most tedious: reviewing all the evidence you have collected.

The evidence review can be a very exciting part of the entire investigating process, depending on your attitude. This is where you get to become a detective, hone your skills for noticing important details, and increase your perceptiveness. It is also the point at which you review hours and hours of video and audio that can often yield nothing at all. However, when you do find something, it makes it all worthwhile. Let's begin by discussing the most effective methods of review.

Always review the evidence with at least one other person. It's most effective to have someone who participated in the investigation as a part of the review team. He or she has a better working knowledge of most of what went on that night and can help you quickly discard false positives.

Remember the notepad and paper we suggested you bring on an investigation? This is a great time to have that handy, so you can cross-reference notes from the investigation while watching the video or viewing photographs. It's good to keep a second notepad handy for the review process, so that when you see or hear something, you can write it down along with what you think may have caused it. At this point, ask your partner to review the same piece of evidence and have her make her own notes. Then compare the two sets of notes. Together, you can try to determine if there's a logical explanation.

If you cannot come up with possible explanations, you may have discovered a very good piece of evidence that you can share with your client or the paranormal community. If you both agree on the fact that it was most likely caused by something non-paranormal in nature, you can just discard it and move on. Or you may want to earmark the evidence to show to the entire team before you completely disregard it. That way, they can weigh in on the final decision.

If you have the time, it is also suggested that you review the video frame by frame. Sometimes images appear briefly and can be overlooked. If you notice movement or

·70·

BILL MURPHY, DOCUMENTARIAN

a change of light on the video, start going through it frame by frame to see if you can view something that may have gone by too fast to see with the naked eye. Bill Murphy, a good friend of ours, is a documentarian. While researching and compiling his documentary *The Stanley Effect: A Piezoelectric Nightmare!,* he caught some amazing evidence on video that appeared on only about two to three frames of footage.

When reviewing EVP, do not share your thoughts on a particular sound file. Write them down and have the other team members listen and write down what they hear as well. If the EVP is not clear or discernible and you can't make out what is being said, just disregard it and move on.

As investigators, we are asked to review people's evidence all the time, especially EVP. Most of the time they consist of some unintelligible mumbling at best, but the investigator will tell us, "It clearly says, 'You must die!'"

During the review, one of us hears "I like pie"; the other hears "Give it a try." However, had we not been told beforehand by the investigator that it says, "You must die," we might not have heard anything even close to that. Those are usually the "C" class of EVP and are not very strong pieces of evidence to share.

Once you have had a chance to go over the hours of video, audio, and photographic evidence you have collected, it's a must to plan a return trip to see if a logical explanation can be made for any of the evidence you have acquired. Reexamining the setting or location in daylight and again at night can lead to a quick dismissal of what seemed like an amazing anomaly.

Be objective when reviewing your evidence. Look at it not through your eyes but through the eyes of the audience you plan to share it with. Remember that your reputation and that of your team is at stake. Always consider the following: What would your thoughts be if someone you didn't know shared this piece of evidence? What questions would you ask?

You know that if you were handed a picture or had an EVP or video played for you of something considered to be paranormal in nature, you would automatically start trying to figure out a logical explanation. Assume that the people you share your evidence with will do the same. Can you answer all their questions objectively and with confidence? Have you taken time to consider all the elements of the piece of evidence? Could it have been caused by a reflection or lens flare? Could it be that the recorder picked up on a baby monitor from next door? Was someone standing outside the perspective of the camera whose reflection could have been caught on a window, TV, or mirror? All of these questions and more should be answered, and with assurance, so that all other possibilities can be discounted before anything is offered up as final evidence.

Do not rush to show your client the evidence you've amassed until you've had a chance to sleep on the results and look at it with fresh eyes. Sometimes we are quick to jump to a conclusion regarding a piece of evidence. After taking a short time away from it, we find that a memory is triggered or a more logical explanation is opened up to us. This is important, because you are representing yourself and your team as professionals and are trying to gain the trust of the client. Snap decisions that are later found to be wrong can make you and your team look bad and therefore limit your chances of being invited back.

Don't be afraid to ask outsiders their thoughts on the evidence you have obtained. Tell them to be honest, then remove your ego from it and allow yourself to be critiqued. This is a very important aspect to evidence review: sometimes we are so close to an investigation and so involved in our own quest to prove the existence of the paranormal that our judgment can be flawed.

One time Dave was handed an envelope full of photographs. He looked at them one by one and saw that they were mostly reflections, dust orbs, and "matrixed" images. He reviewed the final picture and was assured by the investigator that this was the quintessential picture, a full-on apparition. The investigator told him that the final picture was taken in an old steel-mining town that had been abandoned since the mid-1980s and that no living people were there during the time the photograph was taken. She pointed to the doorway of one of the old stores and said with much pride that she managed to capture a photograph of a man standing in the doorway. Dave reviewed the picture and immediately knew what he was looking at. He googled "James Dean cardboard cutout" and quickly found what he was looking for. In the mid-1980s the Coca-Cola Company used famous celebrities like James Dean, Marilyn Monroe, and Elvis in an ad campaign in which they photoshopped a Coke or Diet Coke can into the hands of these celebrities and then gave cardboard standees of the legendary icons to grocery store chains across America. The stores displayed these stands in the aisles.

What she had photographed was a cardboard James Dean display that was visible through the doorway of the store. Dave then sent the image he discovered online to the woman who had taken the photograph. He was amazed when he received the following e-mail response: "I can see how you think that is what you are looking at; however, I know there was nothing present at the time the picture was taken."

Dave did a side-by-side comparison for the woman. He enlarged and cropped her photo to show just the image inside the doorway. He then placed a photo of the James Dean standee next to her picture and began circling over various points of reference for her, including his hair, the jacket he wore, and even the Diet Coke can he held in both pictures. Once again he received an e-mail: "It is obvious to me that you are just not a believer and will not see paranormal activity even if it comes up and slaps you in the face, so I will look for someone more open to the possibilities of the existence of ghosts."

Dave responded as follows: "I appreciate your asking me to look over the picture, and I am sorry that I was unable to give you the answers or validation you hoped for. Upon further review, you very well may be right—that store may be haunted by a cardboard Diet Coke standee of James Dean. Much luck on your search to validate the paranormal."

This woman was so eager to capture evidence and believe in the paranormal that she was willing to overlook anyone else's thoughts on the photographs she had taken. That is quite common in our field. People want to believe so badly that they throw logic to the wind and are willing to accept any dust particle, tummy rumbling, or smudge on a window as proof of the existence of ghosts. Be smarter than that. You've invested a lot of time in this hobby and on the ghost hunt. Don't negate it all with silly or misleading evidence. Had this woman taken the time to return to the site and investigate, we are 100 percent confident that she would have in fact found herself facing the cardboard advertisement and avoided a lot of embarrassment.

CHAPTER THIRTEEN
PUTTING TOGETHER AN INVESTIGATIVE TEAM

So you're ready to ghost-hunt on your own? Now, time out on the dance floor. Your enthusiasm is appreciated, but you can't just pick up an EMF detector and get going. Well, you could, but you probably wouldn't get very far. Ghost hunting is serious business that takes planning and organization. Before setting out, you need a plan.

And a team of investigators. You should never do this alone or on your own.
The first order of business when beginning ghost hunting is to put together a team of people with similar interest in the paranormal to investigate with. Why? The adage of "safety in numbers" comes to mind, but mostly, it's more fulfilling to conduct ghost investigations when you have a team of friends and associates to spread around the many tasks involved in a successful ghost hunt.

You can have a lot of fun forming your group, defining your mission, and getting ready to go out on investigations to haunted locations, historic places, or personal residences. Choosing the right people for your group is pertinent to its success. This isn't the place for cliques, dramas, social status, or ostracization. Everyone who is interested in joining you should have the opportunity. However, make sure that each individual has a specific task that is beneficial to the group's success.

Many of you might find your fellow investigators through groups or organizations of which you're already a member. Maybe you'll find your teammates at school, at church, on your soccer team, or in a study group. Check with your local library to see if they have any reading groups that are looking to expand on their research. Wherever you find these people, make sure that everyone has a healthy interest in the paranormal. It doesn't mean that everyone has to be of the same mindset—that would be a bit scary right there!—but good synergy within the group is important for successful investigations. You don't want a bunch of people who are in it for themselves or trying to make money (a huge no-no!) or be the star of the group. Save the drama for your evening television programs and not for ghost hunting. While you certainly want to have fun during your investigations, this is a serious matter, and you want to make sure that the people you choose for your team will have your back no matter what you encounter.

Chat with your friends; see who among them are interested in really getting involved. This could be a great time to meet other people in your school or social group. Maybe the head cheerleader has a special intuition she's been trying to tap into. What if the president of the chess club has the coolest camera equipment in the school? Or maybe the drum major for the marching band has an incredible ear and would be someone to get involved in your sound recordings. Think outside of your social box to find the right teammates to make your investigations a success.

Try not to have too large a group. You know that old saying about how "too many cooks spoil the broth"? Well, it's true in paranormal groups. The more people you have, the greater the chances are of having personality conflicts, heads knocking, or egos clashing. Nobody wants that. Choose carefully, and then make sure that each team member has a specific responsibility.

Before choosing your team, you'll need to decide what kind of group you're going to form. Are you going to base your research, investigations, and study mostly on the scientific facts you can produce? Or are you going to rely on a psychic or medium to connect with the metaphysical? Do you plan to rely on thermometers, meters, and gauges or on different forms of divination, intuition, and people with psychic gifts? There's no right or wrong answer. It's just how you want to do it. Every ghost-hunting group throughout the world is different when it comes to its approach. A practical approach would be to mix the science and the metaphysical. That way, if you have a sensitive in your group and he's picking up, say, a cold spot, a thermometer can back up the findings. Having your group do a little of this and a little of that helps to keep the investigations interesting and might mean the difference between figuring out if a place is really haunted or not.

Here's an idea for your team's composition. You certainly don't need all of these positions, but it's a comprehensive list that you can fill in with the appropriate people as you see fit:

LEAD INVESTIGATOR

The lead investigator is the person in charge of the group. This is more than likely the founder of the group, who puts everything together. This person should have good leadership and organizational skills and should also be able to delegate in a respectful and deferential manner. This person would serve as the main contact for any clients who use the group's services, and he or she would be responsible for any and all meetings.

BASE-CAMP LEADER

As mentioned in the technology section, base camp is a location set up at each investigation that serves as a home base for informational purposes, as well as where your computer monitors and other measuring equipment reside. A base-camp leader would be responsible for making sure that all the equipment is functioning properly and that team members have all the tools they need for the investigation. This is also a great place to rest, leave your cell phone, get a drink of water or snack, or check on your status. Think of your base-camp leader as the "mother hen" of the group.

PSYCHIC/MEDIUM/SENSITIVE

The famous Hans Holzer, author of *Ghost Hunter,* said once that there are many well-meaning young people who like to do ghost hunting. His advice is simple: Find yourself a good, proven, deep trance medium and work with him or her. The same is true today. (See chapter eight, "The Use of Psychics and Mediums.") So many of us are born with an intuition that often gets squelched before it has a chance to develop. If you have a friend who feels that he has a sensitivity or can see, feel, or hear things that others can't, encourage him to explore his gift through your group. It's also important to have an adult mentor for any young psychic to turn to for advice, experience, and direction.

TECH SPECIALIST

With all the equipment you'll be using in your ghostly investigations, you're going to need someone who's in charge of all it—preferably someone with a good technological head on her shoulders and an interest in wiring, switches, bells, lights, and whistles. Yeah, okay, we'll say it. You need a tech geek. And there's nothing wrong with being a tech geek. Think of the hours your group will save with computer malfunctions, cameras not working, or the site wiring getting crossed up. You'll be glad you have a techie friend on hand to take care of troubleshooting these problems and adding her own special scientific hand to the team.

STILL PHOTOGRAPHER

Check out your school or library's photography club or raid the school's newspaper or yearbook staff and nab yourself a great photographer. While it's true that ghosts and spirits don't just stand in the corner posing and waiting for you to snap the perfect portrait of them, it does bear some truth that someone who is handy with photography equipment is a benefit to any ghost-hunting team. These days, everyone has a digital camera or even quick snap capabilities on his or her cell phone. However, if you choose the right person for your group who has good camera equipment and knows how to use it in infrared or night vision or low light, then imagine the possibilities when it comes to your photographic evidence.

VIDEOGRAPHER

Just as you'll want a good photographer, you might want someone who's dedicated to capturing video of your investigations. If you have someone committed to training an eye around your investigative site and capturing everyone's activities on video, you never know what you'll capture. Small, hand-held recorders can be used by team members, but your videographer should be in charge of the DVDs when it comes time for the evidence review.

EVP SPECIALIST

Chances are that a lot of people on your team will be attempting to collect EVP. It's a good idea, though, to have someone on the team specifically assigned to the EVP and keeping them organized, collected, and stamped with the time and date. This person should have a really good ear. Not like a dog that can hear a high-pitched whistle, but there are some people who are just able to make out words, phrases, and voices when others can't. People who are musically inclined have good ears. Why not ask a band member or someone from the music club into your group? Take advantage of his or her talent while working to capture electronic evidence of the voices of unseen entities.

CLIENT SPECIALIST

You know that one friend you go to with all your troubles? The one person who could earn a psychology degree for all the hours spent listening to and solving everyone else's problems? Don't you want that person on your team? Why? Because when you start your investigations, you're going to be going into the homes of people who are frightened or disturbed by whatever they're experiencing. They may have little kids or pets that are freaked out. They're going to need someone calm, cool, and collected to help liaison their information to your group. This person will also act as a sort of counselor in situations in which a family may need additional help brought in, like a doctor or the clergy. Choose the right person to represent your group to the clients on a one-on-one basis.

RESEARCHER

You're going to encounter more than just spirits in your ghost hunting. A lot of times, noises, smells, situations, etc. in a location come from things other than otherworldly beings—like bad wiring, leaky pipes, loose light bulbs, creaky stairs, or bottles of detergent in hidden cupboards. The list goes on. Every member of your team must take the responsibility of being a researcher and using his or her senses to suss out anything he or she encounters. But you may also want a lead researcher in the group for when you have to go to city hall for registry information, need to find previous owners of homes, or need someone who really knows his or her way around the Internet. Good research is the backbone of any in-depth investigation. The more armed you and your team are with information, the better your results will be.

SKEPTIC

(See chapter eleven, "A Healthy Dose of Skepticism.") In any ghost investigation, there's a tendency to want to believe that everything you hear, see, and feel is paranormal in nature. Sometimes having a grounded skeptic in your group to keep you honest is a great way to bounce around opinions and ideas. We're not talking a cynic, but someone who can genuinely step back, look at a situation, and take a skeptical approach to the evidence that's being gathered and question it in a scientific manner to make sure that no stones are left unturned.

OTHERS

Check with people you know who understand building, electronics, plumbing, and electrical wiring, as they can often shed immediate light on mysterious occurrences like flickering lights, doors swinging open, and banging noises coming from behind walls. Sometimes an expert in these fields can offer a fast and simple explanation of phenomena that are being mistaken for paranormal activity. Also, if you can get in with local law enforcement, it would be a good thing to have a member of the police along with you as a mentor and a protector.

As a teen starting a group, it's good to involve adults in what you're doing, for no other reason than that they're going to worry about you anyway, so why not cut them in from the beginning? Find an adult in the paranormal community who can act as a sponsor or mentor to your group. As mentioned previously, do you know any police officers? They're great go-to people whenever you have questions or concerns. Also, it doesn't hurt to involve a clergy member, like a minister, priest, or even a shaman. It's just smart business to keep you and your fellow investigators protected at all times. If you have adult supervision for your investigations, chances are you'll be able to do them more often and with less hassle.

Now that you have your team in place, you'll want to make sure that everyone is on the same page in terms of how to investigate, where you're going, what you're getting into, etc. Come up with a clever, unifying name for the group. Order T-shirts, sweatshirts, hats, and/or jackets for everyone. Start a website where everyone can go and submit evidence and read up on where you'll be investigating. Or start a blog where all your teammates can contribute. You can even start a Yahoo group specifically for your team, where you'll have a message board of ideas and topics for everyone to discuss.

If you're feeling really industrious, schedule regular meetings for your group, not just when you're out investigating. Topics for discussion could be about the paranormal or what other groups are investigating. You may want to bring speakers in to present the latest technology tools, tips, trends, and topics. Keep the information fresh and interesting so that your team members will keep coming back for more and contributing. Make it fun for everyone involved, even when you're in serious investigator mode.

Now that you've got your team in place, you're probably itching to get going on your first ghost investigation. Question is, where should you go? The possibilities are nearly limitless, as spirits can be practically anywhere. It's all a matter of doing research ahead of time on haunted places where you might get the most activity.

The main thing before going into any investigation is to have permission to be there. Do not go into abandoned buildings or places that are owned by someone. Always plan to have access to the location legitimately.

Here are a few suggestions of places you can investigate:

CEMETERIES

A lot of people like to begin investigating by going to a cemetery. However, it's illegal in most cities and counties to be in a cemetery after dark or past sundown. In many areas, particularly urban ones, cemeteries are hangouts for vagrants, homeless people, drug dealers, and others engaging in criminal activity. For this reason, safety is paramount when investigating a public location that may not be secure. If you and your group are interested in doing this, please remember to check with the authorities and to follow the rules and posted hours at the place you're investigating. We suggest inviting a local police officer along with you for safety's sake. Also, if you do choose to legally investigate a cemetery, be respectful of the dead and their graves. Don't do anything to desecrate the area or provoke the spirits. They were once people too.

BATTLEFIELDS

Throughout the United States, you can find land where battles have taken place, from the Revolution, the Civil War, battles with Indians, and skirmishes explorers experienced. It's thought that in sites such as these, where there were multiple, violent deaths, you'll experience high levels of spirit energy. Think of places like Gettysburg or Manassas or Lexington and Concord. Not that your group will necessarily want to travel to these specific locations, but anywhere a battle has taken place, you're likely to pick up a lot of residual hauntings.

CHURCHES

What more spiritual place to go to investigate than a church? Spirits on the other side might be hanging around a place of worship because they were members and may still be seeking salvation. As with all places, arrange permission from the clergy in charge before setting up your base camp in the church. Also, learn any history of the church, such as any famous (or infamous) parishioners who might come through to you.

HISTORIC LOCALES

Do you live in a town that has historic buildings or locations? Chances are, you do. Because these are typically quite old, it's likely that there are spirits attached to them. Most historic locations also have public access, so you may have a smooth time setting up an investigation with whoever is in charge. Be sure to do your research on who lived and might have died there, what took place, what's significant about the location, whether there were any tragedies in the spot, etc. Be creative and arm yourself with as much information before your investigation as you can. This will help when you're gathering and comparing evidence.

THEATERS

A lot of the paranormal television shows out there have at one time or other visited theaters. These are great places to investigate because of the level of energy that has run through the buildings over the years. Think of the creativity and emotions and humor that came from the performers. Couple that with the energy, participation, and enjoyment of the audience. A lot of psychics say that theaters leave imprints from the people who have been through there. If you have an old theater in your area, this might be a great place to explore, including the stage, the seats, the crew area, the dressing rooms, and even the basement.

SCHOOLS, COLLEGES, AND UNIVERSITIES

Academic locations have a lot of potential for strong psychic energy because of the number of souls that have passed through the corridors over the years. Also, in buildings like these, you're likely to get residual energy from emotional times. If you have a local college or university, research the campus to see if there's any history of paranormal activity. Especially check with the resident halls and dorms. In larger cities, some colleges and universities convert old hotels into housing for their students. Those old hotels might bring with them spiritual guests who never checked out.

HOTELS

Again, think of how many souls have passed through hotels. Emotional energy can be quite high in a hotel as well, when you think about all the events that may have taken place behind closed doors. Some of the most exciting places in the country to explore are old hotels like the Stanley Hotel in Estes Park, Colorado, the Myrtles in St. Francisville, Louisiana, and Mount Washington Hotel in Bretton Woods, New Hampshire. Look around your area for older hotels or even bed-and-breakfasts that come with history attached to them. Some places desperately want proof of hauntings because they can use it in their advertising to attract guests. Surely they'll welcome a ghost-investigation team to help give them evidence.

FORMER NAVY SHIPS

If you live near a national park or near the water, check around for any former U.S. Navy ships that might be docked and available for the public to tour. These vessels have more than likely been through war and hold the energy of the people who passed through the decks. They were also in battles, where lives would have been lost. The potential for spirit energy is great at these locations. As always, make sure you have permission and perhaps a volunteer from the ship to take you around and point out unsafe spots to watch for during your investigation.

ABANDONED HOSPITALS OR PRISONS

Throughout the country, there are closed or abandoned hospitals that were once home to the mentally challenged, the infirm, the sick, and possibly the insane or psychotic. Many closed prisons that harbored criminals over the years are open to tours and the public as well. These places have tremendous potential for hauntings because of the nature of what might have gone on inside the walls. Some well-known places that have been featured on television are Alcatraz, in San Francisco; Eastern State Penitentiary, in Philadelphia; Waverly Hills Sanatorium, in Louisville, Kentucky; and Rolling Hills Paranormal Research Center in Bethany, New York, to name a few. Check in and around your area to see if there are old hospital or prison structures you and your group may get permission to explore and investigate. You could get some very interesting evidence.

PRIVATE HOMES

There are innumerable private homes that get paranormal activity. However, you will need the owners of these residences to contact you and your group directly before you can access their homes. This is where your website and contact information come into play, because people can reach out to you to come and investigate their homes. When you're called in to a situation like this, be respectful of the family and be sure to interview them thoroughly about the type of activity they have been experiencing. Do research on past owners of the house and come armed with information about what may have occurred, not only in the house, but on the land the house stands on. Just because it's a house with a driveway now doesn't mean it wasn't an Indian burial ground a hundred years ago.

OTHER PLACES TO LOOK

In addition to physical structures, you may also want to have your group investigate places where tragedies or tragic deaths occurred. These can be sites of murders, rape, suicide, car wrecks, robberies, shootings, etc. It's thought that often these sites can be haunted by the spirits involved because they may not fully grasp what happened to them and may not have passed on. People have reported ghost cars, ghost ships, and ghost hitchhikers that linger around the areas where people died. These might be great places to measure energy levels, check for EVP, and test your team psychic's ability to pick up residual energy from the events. Another place to check out would be sites of executions or hangings from years past. These have been noted as having hauntings around them. This would take some research on the part of your team, but it would be worth it if you got some exciting evidence. Hangings and executions are some of the most violent deaths and can cause spirits to stick around long past their time.

These are just a few suggestions on where to look for investigation locations for you and your team. Remember to plan ahead and scope out any location in the light of day so you know what you're getting into.

Be cautious and smart and alert at all times, and *always* make sure you have permission to go into a location. Have an adult with you during your investigation and make sure you have emergency numbers for backup in the event anything occurs. Always let someone know where your group will be and for how long in case anyone needs to get in touch with you.

If you've planned an outdoor investigation and it rains or snows, you'll want to reschedule, as the weather conditions won't be conducive to a good investigation.

Be professional, have fun, listen up, get plenty of evidence, and be sure to share it with the owner or proprietor of any of these locations. Document your findings and provide the owners with a copy of your notes and your audio or video files. Most likely you'll be asked back again and/or recommended to other locations where hauntings are occurring.

Conclusion

We hope that this guide has given you the initial insight to understand what paranormal investigation is and, more important, what it is not. In spite of what you see on television, it really isn't that glamorous or even that exciting at times. The work is long, hard, tedious, and repetitive, but it can also be a very rewarding journey. If you are religious or spiritual, discovering evidence of a hidden paranormal world can amplify and accentuate your beliefs. It can be a path of spiritual enlightenment.

We've really only scratched the surface here with this book. We've armed you with the tools and, in our opinion, the minimal amount of information required to conduct your own paranormal investigations and assemble a team of like-minded individuals. However, we've said it before and we'll say it again: there are no experts in this field. There is still much work to be done. You, the next generation of ghost hunters, have an amazing opportunity presented before you to educate the masses, to continue the groundwork that has been laid by legends of the field before you, and to better understand who we are as living beings, what our place is in the universe, and what possibilities there are of an afterlife.

It was our intention from the very beginning for this guide to set you out on the right foot. That is the only thing we can hope for. There are many investigators in the field today who do not represent our field in a positive light. With this guide, we're trying to help you avoid the pitfalls and traps that have ensnared investigators in the past.

KEY WORDS: OPEN MIND, RESPECT, MATURITY, RESPONSIBILITY, INTEGRITY, AND CURIOSITY.

This final chapter doesn't mark the end. Rather, it marks the beginning of what we hope will be a promising and rewarding hobby for you. We want you to know that we are only an e-mail away should you have further questions, concerns, ideas, or just want to drop us a line or a quick hello. We'd love to hear from you. Please understand that due to the volume of e-mails we each receive, a personal response may not always be possible. We will read and make every effort to answer all the e-mail we receive.

However, we do not wish to leave you with unanswered questions with no outlet or resource to turn to. Therefore, we have established www.teenghosthunter.com, where you can ask questions, post ideas, and maybe even make some new friends with similar interests along the way.

With that said, class is dismissed. Build a team and start exploring this fascinating, unseen world around you that may be intertwined with our own.

Best of luck, and happy hunting!
Marley, Patrick, and Dave

Sample Interview Questionnaire

When you start an investigation, one of your first duties is to interview your client. The following is a sample questionnaire that you and your team may use and adapt for your own investigations. This is only a starting guide. It is expected and encouraged that you and your team tailor the questionnaire to your clients' specific needs.

An electronic version of this questionnaire is available on our website at www.teen ghosthunter.com.

1. Address site:

2. Name of witness:

3. Mailing address, if different:

4. Phone number(s):

5. E-mail address:

6. How many occupants are at the location?

7. How many pets are at the location?

8. Names and ages of occupants:

9. Occupations of occupants:

10. Religious beliefs of occupants:

11. How long have the occupants lived at the location?

12. What is the age of the site?

13. How many previous owners have there been? (If known.)

14. What is the history of the site (including tragedies, deaths, and previous complaints)?

15. How many rooms in the site?

16. Has the location been blessed by the clergy?

17. Has there been any recent remodeling? If so, what and where?

18. Are any occupants on prescribed medication for anxiety, depression, pain, etc.? Please list names and medications.

19. Are any occupants using illegal drugs? (This will be kept confidential.)

20. Do any occupants drink alcohol heavily? (This will be kept confidential.)

21. Are any occupants interested in the occult? (Ouija boards, séances, psychics, spells, etc.) If so, who and what?

22. Are any occupants currently seeing a psychiatrist or in therapy? If so, who and why? (This will be kept confidential.)

23. Do any occupants have frequent or unexplained illnesses? If yes, please describe.

24. Have any religious clergy been consulted? If so, please list the names and churches:

25. Have any news media been involved? If so, who?

26. Have there been any witnesses other than the occupants? Please list their names and relationships.

27. Have there been any distinct odors, like perfumes, flowers, sulfur, ammonia, excrement, etc.? If so, what, where, and where?

28. Have there been any sounds of footsteps, knocking, banging, etc.? If so, what was it and when?

29. Have there been any sounds of voices, like whispering, yelling, crying, speaking, etc.? If so, what, where, and when?

30. Have any objects moved? If so, what, where, and when?

31. Have there been any apparitions? If so, what, where, and when? Please describe.

32. Have there been any uncommon hot or cold spots? If so, please describe.

33. Have there been any problems with electrical appliances like the TV, lights, kitchen appliances, doorbell, etc.? If so, what, where, and when?

34. Have there been any problems with the plumbing like leaks, flooding, problems with sinks or toilets, etc.? If so, what, where, and when?

35. Are any occupants having nightmares or trouble sleeping? If so, who, and what are they experiencing?

36. Has there been any physical contact? If so, what happened, where, and with whom?

37. Are there any pets in the household that are affected? If so, please explain.

38. Describe the first occurrence of the phenomena and what happened.

39. Who first witnessed the phenomena?

40. What time of day was the first occurrence of the phenomena?

41. What was the witness's reaction when the phenomena occurred?

42. How long is the average duration of the phenomena?

43. How often do the phenomena occur?

44. Do any of the occupants feel that the phenomena are threatening? If so, who and why?

45. What do the occupants believe is happening? Do they believe it's supernatural or natural, or are they unsure?

46. Do all of the occupants agree on what is happening? Do any of them think it's nonsense or not happening at all?

47. Is there anything new to the house? Any new furniture or items? Anything bought at antique stores or inherited from a deceased relative? If so, what?

48. What would you like to see accomplished from this visit?

Terminology

ANOMALY—something that is not common or normal. In the terms of the paranormal, it can refer to an unusual occurrence of light patterns, strange sounds, abnormal temperatures, etc.

APPARITION—a ghostly figure or a specter.

ASTRAL PROJECTION—a state of being in which a subject feels as if he or she has left his or her physical body. Many times these events occur during sleep, but the subject reports having full conscious awareness of his or her surroundings.

AURA—a field of subtle, luminous radiation supposedly surrounding a person or object like the halo of religious art.

AUTOMATIC WRITING—a process by which an individual places a writing instrument to paper and then, without concentrating on what he or she is writing, allows subconscious thoughts to flow through and guide the pen. This is one of the most basic forms of channeling.

CHANNELING—the process by which a psychic or medium receives messages or information purported to be communications from the spirit world.

CLAIRALIENCE—the ability to smell in a paranormal manner; a form of extrasensory perception in which information comes through the sense of smell.

CLAIRAUDIENCE—the ability to hear in a paranormal manner; a form of extrasensory perception in which information comes by auditory means.

CLAIRCOGNIZANCE—the ability to know in a paranormal manner; a form of extrasensory perception in which information comes by means of intrinsic knowledge.

CLAIRSENTIENCE—the ability to touch or feel in a paranormal manner; a form of extrasensory perception in which information comes by means of feeling.

CLAIRVOYANCE—the ability to get information by means other than the known human extrasensory perception.

CLEANSING—one of several faith-based techniques that are believed to help remove, lessen, or calm paranormal activity.

COLD SPOT—a highly localized space, usually only a few feet in diameter, where the ambient air temperature is markedly colder than the surrounding temperature by several degrees or more.

CYNICISM—sometimes confused with skepticism, a complete dismissal of the possibility of any alleged paranormal activity.

DEMON—a nonhuman, supernatural entity of an evil or malevolent nature.

DOWSING—the practice that attempts to locate hidden water, physical items, energy fields, and spiritual beings without the use of scientific devices. A Y- or L-shaped twig or rods are most commonly used for this purpose, but one may also employ the use of a pendulum.

ECTOPLASM—a substance believed to be the byproduct of the manifestation of spiritual energy.

ELECTROMAGNETIC FIELD METER—otherwise known as an EMF detector. A scientific device that allows one to detect strong fields of electromagnetic radiation. It is believed that a spirit or ghost can either give off or disrupt existing magnetic fields when it is present.

EXTRASENSORY PERCEPTION—also known as ESP. The apparent ability to acquire information by paranormal means independent of the normal five senses (sight, hearing, smell, taste, and touch).

ELECTRONIC VOICE PHENOMENON, -A—also know as EVP. Disembodied voices and sounds captured on audio recording equipment that are believed to be of a paranormal nature.

EXORCISM—a procedure of removing or casting out malevolent spiritual energies from a person or a location that is believed to be possessed.

FALSE POSITIVE—evidence collected on a paranormal investigation that is determined to be caused by non-paranormal events.

FRONT-LOADING—the act of having prior knowledge regarding the history or nature of a specific haunting before conducting an investigation.

GHOST—a spiritual being or entity confined or bound to a specific location, object, or person and believed to have once been a living person itself.

GHOST HUNTER—one who actively seeks out paranormal phenomena believed to be caused by ghosts and spirits.

GHOST HUNTING—the act of scouting or exploring a location in search of spiritual paranormal activity.

GHOST INVESTIGATING—similar to ghost hunting but a much more structured and regimented process that includes gathering and reviewing evidence and writing a detailed report at the investigation's conclusion.

HAUNTING—the visitation or occupation of a person, location, or object by a ghost.

HOT SPOT—a highly localized space, usually only a few feet in diameter, where the ambient air temperature is markedly warmer than the surrounding temperature by several degrees or more.

MATERIALIZATION—the creation or manifestation of matter or spiritual entities from paranormal sources.

MEDIUM—a psychic sensitive who converses directly with spirits or ghosts.

ORB—a visual phenomenon that appears on video and in photographs as a glowing, translucent sphere. Most investigators discount orbs as false positives caused by airborne particles such as dust, pollen, rain, snow, or insects.

OUT-OF-BODY EXPERIENCE—sometimes also knows as astral projection or a flying dream.

PARANORMAL—beyond the present scope of scientific understanding.

PATTERN RECOGNITION—sometimes also called pareidolia, a psychological phenomenon in which the human brain attempts to create order from chaotic or random visual and auditory stimuli. An example would be seeing faces and other identifiable shapes in clouds.

POLTERGEIST—German term translating literally to "noisy ghost." Poltergeist activity is defined as any physical manifestation of a paranormal event. Examples would be objects moving by unseen forces or doors closing or opening on their own. This activity is believed to originate from either spiritual manifestation or involuntary psychokinesis by a living human subject known as a human poltergeist agent, or HAP.

POSSESSION—the control over a human body by supernatural entities.

POSTCOGNITION—the purported psychic knowledge of information about a past event or person.

PRECOGNITION—the perception of information about places or events before they happen.

PSYCHIC—a person who claims to have the ability to perceive information from sources beyond the five known senses.

PSYCHOKINESIS—from a Greek word translating to "movement from the mind," the production or control of motion, especially in inanimate and remote objects, purportedly by the exercise of psychic powers.

SÉANCE—a gathering of individuals for the purpose of attempting to communicate with the spirit world.

SENSITIVE—a blanket term used to describe individuals with various psychic abilities.

SKEPTICISM—the method of reserving judgment before all known facts are presented or understood.

SPIRIT—also known as a free spirit; the soul or essence of being of a deceased individual who has passed from one plane of existence into the next. Unlike a ghost, the spirit is not confined or earthbound to a specific location, object, or person.

SPIRITUALISM—a belief system postulating that spirits or ghosts of the dead can be contacted by the living.

TELEPATHY—the transfer of information, thoughts, and/or feelings between individuals by means other than the five known senses.

TRANCE MEDIUM—a medium who is able to allow spiritual beings to take temporary control or possession of his or her body.

About the Authors

MARLEY GIBSON never saw any ghosts growing up—that she knows of—although she has been on many ghost hunts and has gotten some very interesting pictures, videos, and sound files. One of her videos was featured on A&E's Biography Channel's *My Ghost Story* in October 2008. A lifelong fan of the paranormal, Marley sold her Ghost Huntress series to Houghton Mifflin Harcourt's Graphia Books, the first book of which, *The Awakening,* premiered in May 2009, with *The Guidance* following in October 2009 and *The Reason* in May 2010. She also writes nonfiction, her first book of which, *Christmas Miracles,* coauthored with the *New York Times* best-selling author Cecil Murphey, will be released in October 2009 from St. Martin's Press. She can be found online at www.marleygibson.com, at her blog www.booksboysbuzz.com, or on MySpace at www.myspace.com/mhgibson.

PATRICK BURNS is best known as the star of TruTV's *Haunting Evidence.* He approaches the investigation of paranormal claims from a technological and scientific perspective. He is the founder and director of the Ghost Hounds Paranormal Investigators Network (www.ghosthounds.com) and the organizer and coordinator of GhoStock (www.ghostock.com)—a paranormal enthusiasts' convention held at famously haunted locations around the United States. When not chasing ghosts through haunted houses, he enjoys scuba diving and camping. He lives in Atlanta, Georgia, and can be found online at www.patrick-burns.com or on MySpace at www.myspace.com/ghostgeek.

DAVE SCHRADER has been interested in the paranormal since childhood. His experiences include visitations from a deceased grandmother and other spirits, a Bigfoot encounter, and, a few years ago, a UFO sighting over the skies of Trout Lake, Washington. Given the popularity of the paranormal on TV, in the movies, and in literature, Dave decided to bring his unique views and experiences to radio, where he hosts the successful paranormal talk show *Darkness Radio*, heard Saturday and Sunday nights from nine p.m. to midnight Central Standard Time in Minnesota and streamed live to a worldwide audience from its website, www.darknessradio.com.